Betty Crocker

easy family dinners

Simple Recipes and Fun Ideas to Turn Mealtime into Quality Time

WILEY

Wiley Publishing, Inc.

Published by Wiley Publishing, Inc., Hoboken, NJ

Library of Congress Cataloging-in-Publication Data:

Crocker, Betty.
Betty Crocker easy family dinners : Simple Recipes and Fun Ideas to Turn Mealtime into Quality Time.— 1st ed.
p. cm.
ISBN 0-7645-4418-7 (alk. paper)
1. Quick and easy cookery. I. Title: Easy family dinners. II. Title.
TX833.5.C68496 2004
641.5′55—dc22

2003020224

Manufactured in the United States of America

10 9 8 7 6 5 4 3 2 1

Cover photo: Roasted Pork Chops and Vegetables (page 170)

GENERAL MILLS, INC.

Director, Book and Online Publishing: Kim Walter

Manager, Book Publishing: Lois L. Tlusty

Editor: Cheri A. Olerud

Recipe Development and Testing: Betty Crocker Kitchens

Food Styling: Betty Crocker Kitchens

Photography: General Mills Photo Studios and Kroese Design

WILEY PUBLISHING, INC.

Publisher: Natalie Chapman

Executive Editor: Anne Ficklen

Managing Editor: S. Kristi Hart

Editor: Caroline Schleifer

Senior Production Editor: Jennifer Mazurkie

Cover Design: Paul DiNovo

Interior Design: Edwin Kuo

Interior Layout: Holly Wittenberg

Manufacturing Manager: Kevin Watt

Dear Friends,

At the end of the day, what could be better than gathering the family for a meal to share together? With this cookbook, Betty Crocker can help even the busiest families enjoy the simple pleasures of spending time together.

You can try whatever works best for *your* family. Maybe one night of the week or month you set aside for a family fun **theme night.** You'll find great suggestions for the whole dinner, along with fun, simple Together Time ideas planned for you to make it a breeze.

On nights when you're looking for a little everyday fun, there are tons of together time tips to help you find something creative to do with the kids, from easy cookie decorating to super-simple ideas that keep the little ones busy while you get dinner ready. Let everyone use their imaginations and go for it!

There's always something new and fun to explore with your family. Let Betty Crocker help you make the most of your dinnertime together.

Warmly,

Betty Crocker

Contents

Dinner: a family affair

Remember when you were growing up, there was always one house in the neighborhood where all the kids used to hang out? It may have been a house down the block or next door, but it was the place everyone wanted to go. There were fun things to do, yummy snacks on hand, and if you were lucky, an invitation to stay for dinner. And if you were really lucky, it was your house.

If you have a family today, you know how hard it is to get everyone together for a meal. With school, music lessons and sports, dinner with the family can often take a backseat. This book helps you plan family dinners with great recipes and activities that make dinner together more special and more fun for everyone. Best of all, you'll work together to create something special without extra effort.

Dinners for Better Health

It's no secret: Families who eat dinner together eat better. The more parents know about health and nutrition, the more healthful are their children's diets. Studies suggest:

Children: **Kids who eat dinner with their families eat more fruits and vegetables and less fat, soda and fried foods. They also get more fiber, vitamins and minerals and tend to eat more healthy even away from home.**

Adults: **Women who eat out at least five meals a week consume more calories and fat than women who dine at home, eating 2,059 calories versus 1,769 calories per day. They often consume a larger proportion of their calories as fat, 35 versus 31 percent.**

Why the difference? **The dinner table shapes good eating habits and homemade meals tend to be more wholesome than restaurant or takeout foods. They are usually lower in fat and contain more vitamins and minerals. When families eat together, healthy eating is often a topic of conversation, and the lessons learned can have lasting impact.**

Keep Dinner Special

In the kitchen, your family can connect and share the day over a meal. Here are simple ways:

Serve wholesome meals your family loves. **Every family has tried-and-true favorites, but it's fun to try new recipes when time allows. A great reason for cooking at home is to include fruits, vegetables and whole grains—ingredients that are often missing in takeout and restaurant meals.**

Get the crew involved. **From preparation to cleanup, it's all hands on deck! Whether mixing or sprinkling, setting the table or cleaning up, including the family in meal preparation is a great way for all to feel they've helped make a part of their meal.**

Share your day. **Take turns sharing the best, most memorable or most important part of the day. Take time to smell the dinner, give thanks and reflect on special moments.**

Turn on the conversation. **Mealtime is one of the rare times families can catch up with each other, so make every moment count by talking and listening.**

Turn off the TV and turn on the answering machine. **Don't let interruptions from the telephone, television or doorbell spoil the fun. Give everyone a break from answering the phone by letting the machine do its work.**

Be flexible about where you eat. **Given family schedules, sitting down at the table may not always be possible. Consider packing a picnic to eat together before sports practice, or plan a meal to eat in the car on the way to music lessons.**

Making Dinnertime Family Time

It's a natural: **Dinnertime + Family Time = Together Time**. Start by making the dinner itself a simple activity for the whole family, one where everyone can do something to help and feel good in the process. For example, Mom selects the recipes and shops, Dad grills, older kids chop vegetables and younger kids mix. You'll create memories that will not be forgotten.

Whenever possible, involve the kids in food adventures such as a family trip to a farmers' market or roadside stand, and let them each pick out a new fruit or vegetable. You'll help your kids taste new foods and have fun at the same time. Another way to let kids know you appreciate their viewpoint is to let them help plan the week's menu and shop for groceries with you to pick up the dinner ingredients.

Knowing how to cook is an important life skill. Cooking with Mom or Dad helps instill confidence and a sense of accomplishment. Children can see, taste and share, with pride, the results of their efforts. Having your kids participate in planning and preparing meals is more than just a way to spend time together and get chores done; it's also a good way to develop and reinforce skills such as reading, counting, measuring, timing, fine motor coordination and teamwork. Plus, chances are they'll open up and talk about other things happening in their lives, such as a new friend in class or a favorite book or sport.

And there are even more benefits. If children are involved with the meal, they'll be more likely to eat what they've helped prepare and to try new foods. Cooking is also an ideal way to introduce and teach children about diverse cultures, new ingredients, nutrition and the value of eating different kinds of foods. Parents play the most important role in helping kids learn how to develop the healthful eating habits that will last a lifetime.

Gather 'Round the Table

Eating together as a family can give everyone a greater appreciation for food, how it's cooked and what it takes to prepare it. Food nourishes and comforts, and just as important, the bonding that happens over a meal nurtures and supports the whole family. For many families, the kitchen is the heart of the home—the place where everyone goes, not just to eat, but also for sharing, learning and growing together. The kitchen and the dinner table are familiar, friendly places where some of the earliest memories and fondest moments have taken place. Many family and neighborhood events and celebrations center around food and become part of the emotional ties that connect generations and even communities.

Experience all the good times and memorable moments that come with cooking dinner and sharing a simple activity with your family. Cooking and eating dinner together is a happy, wholesome way to create homemade fun!

Kids in the Kitchen

While you're busy preparing dinner, let the kids experiment and enjoy the process of making something to eat. To keep "Is dinner ready yet?" questions to a minimum, entertain younger kids with one of these instant-art projects:

Set-the-Table Place Mats: **Offer crayons, markers and place-mat-size paper. Let the kids draw where the plate, cup, glass, fork, knife and spoon go, while they learn how to set the table.**

Create a Bookmark: **Cut pictures from used greeting cards and magazines, glue them onto the front and back of a strip of construction paper.**

Color a Lunch Bag: **Decorate a week or two's supply of white or brown paper lunch bags with markers, crayons, glue sticks, stickers and glitter.**

String Colorful Pasta: **Make a bracelet or necklace by stringing colorful hollow pasta onto yarn. Remember to be on hand to tie it when it's ready.**

Create a Collage: **Use cut-out or torn-out pictures from magazines and used greeting cards to create pictures of a favorite place, a dream room or a family vacation everyone would like to take.**

Write a Story: **Staple together several sheets of blank paper. Let the kids write and illustrate, then read their stories after dinner.**

Make Your Own Music: **Place a square piece of waxed paper over the end of an empty paper-towel tube, and secure it in place with tape or a rubber band. Let the kids hum their favorite tunes into the tube.**

Chapter 1

Schoolnight Meals in 30 Minutes

You're racing. First, it's home from work. Next, without even stopping to change your clothes, it's dinner. Oops, you have to be out the door again in 60 minutes, including feeding hungry mouths. Relax, this chapter's got you covered. Choose any of these easy recipes that the kids will love, made with ingredients you're sure to have on hand, and you can truly be out the door in an hour flat.

Bacon Cheeseburger Pizza
(page 12)

Bacon Cheeseburger Pizza

Photo on page 11

8 SERVINGS PREP: 10 MIN BAKE: 15 MIN

1 loaf (1 pound) unsliced French bread

1 pound ground beef

1 medium onion, chopped (1/2 cup)

1 jar (14 ounces) pizza sauce (any variety)

1 large tomato, seeded and chopped (1 cup)

8 slices bacon, crisply cooked and crumbled

2 cups finely shredded pizza cheese blend (mozzarella and Cheddar cheeses) (8 ounces)

1. Heat oven to 400°. Cut bread loaf horizontally in half. Cut bread halves crosswise in half to make 4 pieces (to fit on cookie sheet). Arrange on large ungreased cookie sheet.
2. Cook beef and onion in 10-inch skillet over medium-high heat about 8 minutes, stirring occasionally, until beef is brown; drain. Stir in pizza sauce. Spread beef mixture over bread. Sprinkle with tomato, bacon and cheese.
3. Bake 12 to 15 minutes or until pizza is hot and cheese is melted.

1 SERVING: Calories 430 (Calories from Fat 200); Fat 22g (Saturated 10g); Cholesterol 60mg; Sodium 860mg; Carbohydrate 35g (Dietary Fiber 3g); Protein 26g • % Daily Value: Vitamin A 14%; Vitamin C 12%; Calcium 24%; Iron 18% • Exchanges: 2 Starch, 1 Vegetable, 3 Medium-Fat Meat, 1/2 Fat • Carbohydrate Choices: 2

together time

Shake, rattle 'n roll! Play your favorite CD, tape or album. Take turns waltzing, jitterbugging, polkaing or moving around the room to the latest dance number.

Orange Teriyaki Beef with Noodles

4 SERVINGS PREP: 5 MIN COOK: 15 MIN

1 pound beef boneless sirloin

1 can (14 ounces) beef broth

1/4 cup teriyaki stir-fry sauce

2 tablespoons orange marmalade

Dash of ground red pepper (cayenne)

1 1/2 cups frozen sugar snap peas (from 1-pound bag)

1 1/2 cups uncooked fine egg noodles (3 ounces)

1. Cut beef into thin strips (beef is easier to cut if partially frozen, about 1 1/2 hours). Spray 12-inch skillet with cooking spray; heat over medium-high heat. Cook beef in skillet about 4 minutes, stirring occasionally, until brown. Remove beef from skillet; keep warm.
2. Mix broth, stir-fry sauce, marmalade and red pepper in skillet. Heat to boiling. Stir in peas and noodles; reduce heat to medium. Cover and cook about 5 minutes or until noodles are tender.
3. Stir beef into noodle mixture. Cook uncovered 2 to 3 minutes or until sauce is slightly thickened.

1 SERVING: Calories 260 (Calories from Fat 45); Fat 5g (Saturated 2g); Cholesterol 80mg; Sodium 1210mg; Carbohydrate 27g (Dietary Fiber 2g); Protein 29g • % Daily Value: Vitamin A 4%; Vitamin C 20%; Calcium 4%; Iron 24% • Exchanges: 2 Starch, 3 Very Lean Meat • Carbohydrate Choices: 2

together time

Learn mealtime math. Let the kids measure ingredients for recipes to show how important math is in everyday life, as well as to teach them how to cook!

Meat and Potato Skillet

4 SERVINGS PREP: 5 MIN COOK: 15 MIN

1 pound beef boneless sirloin

1 tablespoon vegetable oil

1 teaspoon garlic pepper

1 bag (1 pound) frozen potatoes, carrots, celery and onions

1 jar (12 ounces) beef gravy

1. Cut beef into thin strips (beef is easier to cut if partially frozen, about 1 1/2 hours). Heat oil and garlic pepper in 10-inch nonstick skillet over medium-high heat. Cook beef in oil about 4 minutes, stirring occasionally, until brown.
2. Stir in frozen vegetables and gravy; reduce heat to medium. Cover and simmer 7 to 9 minutes, stirring occasionally, until vegetables are tender.

1 SERVING: Calories 275 (Calories from Fat 80); Fat 9g (Saturated 3g); Cholesterol 65mg; Sodium 580mg; Carbohydrate 20g (Dietary Fiber 3g); Protein 28g • % Daily Value: Vitamin A 100%; Vitamin C 6%; Calcium 4%; Iron 18% • Exchanges: 1 Starch, 1 Vegetable, 3 1/2 Very Lean Meat, 1 Fat • Carbohydrate Choices: 1

together time

Share a story. Kids love hearing about what life was like when you were a child. Tell them a story during dinner about your favorite activity or a memorable summer vacation when you were growing up.

Meat and Potato Skillet

Easy Southwestern Stroganoff

4 SERVINGS PREP: 8 MIN COOK: 15 MIN

1 pound ground beef

1 cup water

1 jar (16 ounces) thick-and-chunky salsa

2 cups uncooked wagon wheel pasta (4 ounces)

1/2 teaspoon salt

1/2 cup sour cream

1. Cook beef in 10-inch skillet over medium-high heat about 8 minutes, stirring occasionally, until brown; drain.
2. Stir water, salsa, pasta and salt into beef. Heat to boiling; reduce heat. Cover and simmer about 15 minutes, stirring occasionally, until pasta is tender.
3. Stir in sour cream. Cook just until hot.

1 SERVING: Calories 415 (Calories from Fat 200); Fat 22g (Saturated 10g); Cholesterol 85mg; Sodium 850mg; Carbohydrate 30g; (Dietary Fiber 3g); Protein 27g • % Daily Value: Vitamin A 20%; Vitamin C 12%; Calcium 6%; Iron 22% • Exchanges: 2 Starch, 3 Medium-Fat Meat, 1 Fat • Carbohydrate Choices: 2

together time

Walk the dog. After dinner, gather the entire family and take the dog on a walk. Don't have a dog? Take a walk together anyway.

Barbecue Beef and Corn Shepherd's Pie

6 SERVINGS PREP: 10 MIN COOK: 10 MIN STAND: 10 MIN

1 pound ground beef

8 medium green onions, sliced (1/2 cup)

1 cup barbecue sauce

1 can (11 ounces) whole kernel corn with red and green peppers, drained

1 can (4 1/2 ounces) chopped green chiles, undrained

1/2 package (7-ounce size) Cheddar and bacon mashed potatoes mix (1 pouch)

1 1/2 cups hot water

1/3 cup milk

2 tablespoons butter or margarine

1/2 cup shredded Cheddar cheese (2 ounces)

1 cup corn chips

1. Cook beef and 1/4 cup of the onions in 10-inch nonstick skillet over medium-high heat about 8 minutes, stirring occasionally, until beef is brown; drain well. Stir in barbecue sauce, 3/4 cup of the corn and the chiles. Heat to boiling; reduce heat to low to keep warm.
2. Meanwhile, cook potatoes as directed on package for 4 servings, using 1 pouch Potatoes and Seasoning, hot water, milk and butter. Stir in remaining onions and corn; let stand 5 minutes.
3. Spoon potatoes onto center of beef mixture; sprinkle cheese over potatoes and beef mixture. Cover and let stand about 5 minutes or until cheese is melted. Sprinkle corn chips around edge of skillet.

1 SERVING: Calories 435 (Calories from Fat 180); Fat 20g (Saturated 9g); Cholesterol 65mg; Sodium 910mg; Carbohydrate 44g (Dietary Fiber 4g); Protein 20g • % Daily Value: Vitamin A 16%; Vitamin C 20%; Calcium 12%; Iron 14% • Exchanges: 3 Starch, 2 Medium-Fat Meat, 1 Fat • Carbohydrate Choices: 3

together time

Create a collage. Cut out pictures, words and letters from old magazines to make a collage of family members' dream vacations, their favorite things or their perfect room.

Cheesy Pasta, Veggies and Beef

4 SERVINGS   PREP: 10 MIN   COOK: 10 MIN

1 pound ground beef

1 bag (1 pound) frozen pasta, broccoli, corn and carrots in garlic-seasoned sauce

1 can (10 3/4 ounces) condensed Cheddar cheese soup

1/2 cup water

Macaroni and cheese-flavored cheese topping or cheese-flavored tiny fish-shaped crackers, if desired

1. Cook beef in 10-inch skillet over medium heat about 8 minutes, stirring occasionally, until brown; drain.
2. Stir frozen pasta and vegetable mixture, soup and water into beef. Heat to boiling; reduce heat. Cover and simmer 5 to 7 minutes, stirring occasionally, until vegetables are tender. Sprinkle with cheese topping.

1 SERVING: Calories 320 (Calories from Fat 200); Fat 22g (Saturated 9g); Cholesterol 75mg; Sodium 740mg; Carbohydrate 6g (Dietary Fiber 0g); Protein 24g • % Daily Value: Vitamin A 32%; Vitamin C 0%; Calcium 6%; Iron 10% • Exchanges: 1 Vegetable, 3 High-Fat Meat • Carbohydrate Choices: 1/2

together time

Share your day. Get the conversation rolling. Ask everyone at the table to take turns saying two things that happened today that really made the day special.

Cheesy Pasta, Veggies and Beef

Sloppy Joes Hot Potato Stuffers

4 POTATOES PREP: 7 MIN MICROWAVE: 16 MIN STAND: 5 MIN

4 medium baking potatoes

2 cups Sloppy Joes (page 108), thawed if frozen or 1 can (15 to 16 ounces) chili

1 cup shredded Cheddar cheese (4 ounces)

Sour cream, if desired

Bacon flavor bits, if desired

Chopped onion, if desired

Chopped green bell pepper, if desired

Sliced ripe olives, if desired

1. Pierce potatoes with sharp knife. Arrange potatoes in spoke pattern with narrow ends in center on microwavable paper towel in microwave oven. Microwave on High 12 to 14 minutes, turning once, until tender. Cover and let stand 5 minutes.
2. Cut slit in each potato two-thirds of the way to bottom; gently press ends together to create a "well." Place potatoes on microwavable plate. Top potatoes with Sloppy Joes and cheese. Microwave 1 to 2 minutes or until cheese is melted. Serve with remaining ingredients as toppings.

1 POTATO: Calories 435 (Calories from Fat 205); Fat 23g (Saturated 11g); Cholesterol 85mg; Sodium 1000mg; Carbohydrate 30g (Dietary Fiber 2g); Protein 27g • % Daily Value: Vitamin A 12%; Vitamin C 20%; Calcium 18%; Iron 14% • Exchanges: 2 Starch, 3 Medium-Fat Meat, 1 Fat • Carbohydrate Choices: 2

together time

Sprout a potato. Place an extra raw potato in a glass of water and set it on the windowsill or counter. Over the next few weeks, keep the glass filled and everyone can observe how the potato sprouts and changes.

Take-It-Easy Noodle Dinner

4 SERVINGS PREP: 10 MIN COOK: 8 MIN

1 pound ground turkey or lean ground beef

1 medium onion, coarsely chopped (1/2 cup)

1 cup water

1 can (14 1/2 ounces) stewed tomatoes, undrained

1 package (10 ounces) frozen green peas, thawed and drained

1 package (3 ounces) chicken-flavor or beef-flavor ramen noodle soup mix

1. Cook turkey and onion in 12-inch nonstick skillet over medium heat about 8 minutes, stirring occasionally, until turkey is no longer pink; drain.
2. Stir water, tomatoes, peas and seasoning packet from soup mix into turkey. Break up noodles; stir into turkey mixture. Heat to boiling, stirring occasionally; reduce heat. Cover and simmer about 6 minutes, stirring occasionally to separate noodles, until noodles are tender.

1 SERVING: Calories 310 (Calories from Fat 90); Fat 10g (Saturated 2g); Cholesterol 75mg; Sodium 690mg; Carbohydrate 29g (Dietary Fiber 5g); Protein 31g • % Daily Value: Vitamin A 14%; Vitamin C 16%; Calcium 6%; Iron 16% • Exchanges: 1 1/2 Starch, 1 Vegetable, 3 1/2 Very Lean Meat, 1 Fat • Carbohydrate Choices: 2

together time

Dress up your table. Make a bouquet of dandelions or clover from the bunch that your child picked for you today. Your little one will feel honored to have this gift displayed so prominently!

Cincinnati Chili

6 SERVINGS PREP: 10 MIN COOK: 16 MIN

- 10 ounces uncooked spaghetti
- 1 tablespoon vegetable oil
- 1 pound ground turkey breast
- 1 medium onion, chopped (1/2 cup)
- 1 clove garlic, finely chopped
- 1 jar (26 to 28 ounces) chunky vegetable-style tomato pasta sauce
- 1 can (15 to 16 ounces) kidney beans, rinsed and drained
- 2 tablespoons chili powder
- 1/2 cup shredded Cheddar cheese (2 ounces), if desired
- 3 medium green onions, sliced, if desired

1. Cook and drain spaghetti as directed on package.
2. While spaghetti is cooking, heat oil in 10-inch skillet over medium heat. Cook turkey, onion and garlic in oil about 6 minutes, stirring occasionally, until turkey is no longer pink.
3. Stir in pasta sauce, beans and chili powder; reduce heat. Simmer uncovered 10 minutes, stirring occasionally. Serve sauce over spaghetti. Sprinkle with cheese and green onions.

1 SERVING: Calories 510 (Calories from Fat 110); Fat 12g (Saturated 2g); Cholesterol 50mg; Sodium 850mg; Carbohydrate 80g (Dietary Fiber 9g); Protein 32g • % Daily Value: Vitamin A 34%; Vitamin C 18%; Calcium 8%; Iron 32% • Exchanges: 5 Starch, 2 Lean Meat • Carbohydrate Choices: 5

together time

When the weather outside is frightful, make indoor s'mores. Layer chocolate bars and marshmallows between graham crackers on a microwavable napkin. Microwave on High 10 to 15 seconds or until marshmallows are a little melted and chocolate is warm.

Cincinnati Chili

Penne with Cheesy Tomato Sauce

5 SERVINGS PREP: 5 MIN COOK: 12 MIN

2 2/3 cups uncooked penne pasta (8 ounces)

1/2 pound bulk Italian pork sausage

1 container (15 ounces) refrigerated tomato pasta sauce

1/4 cup shredded fresh basil leaves

1/2 cup diced mozzarella cheese (2 ounces)

1/4 cup shredded fresh Parmesan cheese (1 ounce)

1. Cook and drain pasta as directed on package.
2. While pasta is cooking, cook sausage in 3-quart saucepan over medium heat about 8 minutes, stirring occasionally, until no longer pink; drain.
3. Stir pasta sauce into sausage. Heat to boiling; reduce heat to medium-low. Stir in basil and mozzarella cheese. Cook 1 to 2 minutes or until cheese is slightly melted. Serve sauce over pasta. Sprinkle with Parmesan cheese.

1 SERVING: Calories 430 (Calories from Fat 145); Fat 16g (Saturated 6g); Cholesterol 35mg; Sodium 880mg; Carbohydrate 52g (Dietary Fiber 3g); Protein 19g • % Daily Value: Vitamin A 16%; Vitamin C 10%; Calcium 18%; Iron 16% • Exchanges: 3 Starch, 1 Vegetable, 1 1/2 High-Fat Meat • Carbohydrate Choices: 3

together time

Declare a special night for each family member. Have everyone at the table say what's great about the "distinguished" person.

Sausage Skillet Supper

6 SERVINGS PREP: 5 MIN COOK: 20 MIN

3 tablespoons vegetable oil

1 bag (24 ounces) frozen diced potatoes with onions and peppers

1/2 teaspoon dried oregano or basil leaves

1/2 teaspoon pepper

2 cups broccoli flowerets

1 ring (about 3/4 pound) bologna or smoked sausage

3 slices process American cheese, cut diagonally in half

1. Heat oil in 10-inch skillet over medium-high heat. Add potatoes, oregano and pepper. Cover and cook 8 to 10 minutes, stirring occasionally, until potatoes are light brown.
2. Stir in broccoli; add bologna. Cover and cook about 10 minutes or until bologna is hot. Top with cheese. Cover until cheese is melted.

1 SERVING: Calories 360 (Calories from Fat 225); Fat 25g (Saturated 9g); Cholesterol 40mg; Sodium 750mg; Carbohydrate 23g (Dietary Fiber 3g); Protein 11g • % Daily Value: Vitamin A 12%; Vitamin C 34%; Calcium 8%; Iron 36% • Exchanges: 1 Starch, 1 Vegetable, 1 High-Fat Meat, 3 1/2 Fat • Carbohydrate Choices: 1 1/2

together time

Let the kids plan dinner once in a while. Discuss ideas, and let them choose tonight's meal. It helps kids feel in control of what they're eating, and they may be more willing to try something new.

family fun
ITALIAN NIGHT

Mangia! (pronounced MON-ja). That's Italian for "Eat!" and that's what your family will love to do when you make an Italian meal together. Pasta is always popular in Italy but there are plenty of other options to try. Raise your glasses and toast each other with "salute" (pronounced sa-LOOT-eh) tonight.

Menu

Cheesy Italian Ravioli *(page 142)*

Shake Salad (at right)

Sesame Seed Fingers (at right) or purchased breadsticks

Brownie Pizza (at right)

Shake Salad

In a large resealable plastic food-storage bag, layer 1/2 cup **creamy Italian dressing**, 1/2 cup **shredded Cheddar cheese** or pizza blend cheese, 1/2 cup **shredded carrots** and 4 cups torn **salad greens**. Seal bag, and shake to toss salad.

Sesame Seed Fingers

Set oven control to broil. Spread 3 tablespoons **butter** over 6 slices **whole wheat bread**; sprinkle with 1 tablespoon **sesame seed** or poppy seed. Cut each slice crosswise into 4 strips; place strips in broiler pan. Broil with tops 4 inches from heat 1 1/2 to 2 minutes or until edges of bread are brown.

Brownie Pizza

Heat oven to 350°. Grease 12-inch pizza pan. Make 1 package (19.8 ounces) **fudge brownie mix**, using amounts of **water**, **oil** and **eggs** called for on package. Spread batter in pan. Bake 23 to 25 minutes or until toothpick inserted 2 inches from side of pan comes out clean or almost clean. Let cool 1 to 2 hours. Frost with **frosting**, and decorate with **candy sprinkles** or other colored candies. Cut in wedges.

More Italian Ideas

Ready for a change from ravioli? Try these other Italian dishes instead.

Italian Garden Frittata (page 52)
Rigatoni Pizza Stew (page 144)
Italian Beef Stew (page 114)
Mini Italian Meat Loaves (page 167)

helping is fun

Mom or Dad

- Makes the ravioli
- Heats oven to broil
- Cuts bread slices into strips

The Kids

- Make and shake salad
- Butter bread and sprinkle with seeds
- Mix brownies; spread in pan

together time

Personalize your pizza. After dinner, get everyone together to frost and decorate the brownie pizza. (Try red, white and green frosting!) Serve wedges with a big glass of milk.

Learn about different foods. When serving ravioli, ask, "What are some other kinds of pasta?" and "What dishes were created in Italy and then became popular in the U.S.?"

Spur the kids' interest in Italy and its regions. What are some of the cities in Italy? What's the capital? Have an atlas or travel guide handy to look up the answers.

Read an Italian storybook. There are some great kids' books that describe and picture various regions of Italy. After dinner, read *Strega Nona* by Tomie dePaola or *Angelo* by David Macaulay.

Easy Beans and Franks Soup

6 SERVINGS PREP: 10 MIN COOK: 15 MIN

1 can (28 ounces) baked beans with bacon and brown sugar sauce, undrained

1 can (11 1/2 ounces) eight-vegetable or tomato juice

6 franks, cut into 1-inch slices

3 medium carrots, chopped (1 1/2 cups)

1 large onion, chopped (1 cup)

1 clove garlic, finely chopped

1 teaspoon Worcestershire sauce

1. Mix all ingredients in 2-quart saucepan.
2. Heat to boiling; reduce heat. Simmer uncovered 10 to 15 minutes or until carrots are tender.

1 SERVING: Calories 420 (Calories from Fat 190); Fat 21g (Saturated 8g); Cholesterol 40mg; Sodium 970mg; Carbohydrate 49g (Dietary Fiber 5g); Protein 15g • % Daily Value: Vitamin A 100%; Vitamin C 18%; Calcium 10%; Iron 18% • Exchanges: 3 Starch, 1/2 High-Fat Meat, 1 Vegetable, 2 1/2 Fat • Carbohydrate Choices: 3

together time

Practice listening. Bone up on listening skills with your kids at mealtime. "Sounds like you had a fun day," or "Wow! You really liked that class," lets them know that you're listening and want to know how their day was.

Creamy Chicken-Pasta Stew

4 SERVINGS   PREP: 5 MIN   COOK: 20 MIN

1 tablespoon butter or margarine

1 pound boneless, skinless chicken breasts, cut into 1-inch pieces

1 cup milk

1 package (3 ounces) cream cheese, softened

1 bag (1 pound) frozen pasta, broccoli and carrots in creamy Cheddar sauce

2 tablespoons chopped fresh chives

1. Melt butter in 12-inch nonstick skillet over medium-high heat. Cook chicken in butter 4 to 5 minutes, stirring occasionally, until brown.
2. Stir milk and cream cheese into chicken. Cook about 5 minutes, stirring frequently, until cheese is melted.
3. Stir in frozen pasta and vegetable mixture. Heat to boiling, stirring occasionally; reduce heat. Cover and simmer 3 to 7 minutes or until pasta and vegetables are tender. Sprinkle with chives.

1 SERVING: Calories 410 (Calories from Fat 180); Fat 20g (Saturated 11g); Cholesterol 130mg; Sodium 340mg; Carbohydrate 26g (Dietary Fiber 2g); Protein 34g • % Daily Value: Vitamin A 100%; Vitamin C 10%; Calcium 20%; Iron 12% • Exchanges: 2 Starch, 4 Lean Meat, 1 Fat • Carbohydrate Choices: 2

together time

Fill your cookie jar. Cut refrigerated sugar cookie dough, or another favorite flavor, into various shapes with cookie cutters and bake. The cookies will be ready in about 20 minutes.

Cheesy Chicken Skillet Dinner

6 SERVINGS PREP: 15 MIN COOK: 10 MIN

1 teaspoon vegetable oil

1 1/4 pounds boneless, skinless chicken breasts, cut into 3/4-inch pieces

2 large carrots, cut into 1/8-inch slices (2 cups)

1 medium zucchini, cut into 1/8-inch slices (2 cups)

2 tablespoons soy sauce

8 medium green onions, sliced (1/2 cup)

2 cups shredded sharp reduced-fat Cheddar cheese (8 ounces)

1. Heat 12-inch nonstick skillet over medium-high heat. Add oil; rotate skillet to coat bottom. Add chicken; stir-fry about 5 minutes or until no longer pink in center. Remove from skillet.
2. Add carrots and zucchini to skillet; stir-fry 4 to 5 minutes or until crisp-tender. Add chicken and soy sauce; toss until chicken and vegetables are coated with soy sauce.
3. Sprinkle with onions and cheese. Cover skillet until cheese is melted.

1 SERVING: Calories 205 (Calories from Fat 65); Fat 7g (Saturated 3g); Cholesterol 65mg; Sodium 730mg; Carbohydrate 6g (Dietary Fiber 2g); Protein 31g • % Daily Value: Vitamin A 100%; Vitamin C 6%; Calcium 30%; Iron 8% • Exchanges: 1 Vegetable, 4 Very Lean Meat, 1 Fat • Carbohydrate Choices: 1/2

together time

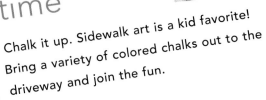

Chalk it up. Sidewalk art is a kid favorite! Bring a variety of colored chalks out to the driveway and join the fun.

Cantonese Chicken Chop Suey

5 SERVINGS PREP: 10 MIN COOK: 20 MIN

1 cup uncooked regular long-grain rice

1 pound boneless, skinless chicken breast halves

1/2 teaspoon peppered seasoned salt

1 bag (1 pound) fresh stir-fry vegetables (4 cups)

1/2 cup water

1/2 cup stir-fry sauce

1 tablespoon honey

2 cups chow mein noodles

1/4 cup cashew pieces

1. Cook rice as directed on package.
2. While rice is cooking, cut chicken into 1/2-inch pieces. Spray 12-inch nonstick skillet with cooking spray; heat over medium-high heat. Add chicken; sprinkle with seasoned salt. Stir-fry 4 to 6 minutes or until brown.
3. Add vegetables and water to skillet. Heat to boiling; reduce heat to medium. Cover and cook 5 to 7 minutes, stirring occasionally, until vegetables are crisp-tender. Stir in stir-fry sauce and honey; heat through.
4. Divide rice and noodles among bowls. Top with chicken mixture. Sprinkle with cashews.

1 SERVING: Calories 435 (Calories from Fat 110); Fat 12g (Saturated 2g); Cholesterol 55mg; Sodium 1460mg; Carbohydrate 58g (Dietary Fiber 4g); Protein 29g • % Daily Value: Vitamin A 100%; Vitamin C 36%; Calcium 8%; Iron 26% • Exchanges: 3 Starch, 2 Vegetable, 4 Lean Meat • Carbohydrate Choices: 4

together time

Mix things up for a little excitement on Wacky Wednesday. Serve dessert first, and pour your beverage into bowls to sip through straws. Have family members wear sunglasses or eat with their mittens on!

Chicken and Corn Bread Stuffing Casserole

4 SERVINGS PREP: 15 MIN BAKE: 15 MIN

1 can (10 3/4 ounces) condensed cream of chicken or celery soup

3/4 cup milk

1 package (10 ounces) frozen mixed vegetables, thawed and drained

1 medium onion, finely chopped (1/2 cup)

1/2 teaspoon ground sage or poultry seasoning

2 cooked chicken breasts from Baked Oregano Chicken (page 171), cut up, or 2 cups cut-up cooked chicken

1 1/2 cups corn bread stuffing mix

1/8 teaspoon pepper

Paprika, if desired

1. Heat oven to 400°. Spray 3-quart casserole with cooking spray.
2. Heat soup and milk to boiling in 3-quart saucepan over high heat, stirring frequently. Stir in mixed vegetables, onion and sage. Heat to boiling, stirring frequently; remove from heat.
3. Stir in chicken and stuffing mix. Spoon into casserole. Sprinkle with pepper and paprika. Bake uncovered about 15 minutes or until hot in center.

1 SERVING: Calories 300 (Calories from Fat 80); Fat 9g (Saturated 3g); Cholesterol 45mg; Sodium 1020mg; Carbohydrate 34g (Dietary Fiber 4g); Protein 21g • % Daily Value: Vitamin A 48%; Vitamin C 20%; Calcium 12%; Iron 12% • Exchanges: 2 Starch, 1 Vegetable, 2 Very Lean Meat, 1 Fat • Carbohydrate Choices: 2

together time

Make grape poppers. Have the kids rinse grape clusters, then dip into sugar. Place the grapes in the freezer while you're making dinner. They'll be a frosty, fun treat for dessert!

Chicken and Corn Bread Stuffing Casserole

Double-Cheese Chicken Caesar Pizza

8 SERVINGS PREP: 10 MIN BAKE: 15 MIN

1 package (10 ounces) ready-to-serve thin Italian pizza crust (12 inches in diameter)

1/4 cup creamy Caesar dressing

1 cup shredded mozzarella or provolone cheese (4 ounces)

16 to 18 frozen fully cooked breaded mozzarella cheese nuggets (from 13 1/2-ounce package)

1 package (9 ounces) frozen smoke-flavor fully cooked chicken breast strips

1/4 cup sliced ripe olives

1 small red bell pepper, cut into thin strips

1/3 cup grated Parmesan cheese

1. Heat oven to 450°. Place pizza crust on ungreased cookie sheet.
2. Spread dressing evenly on pizza crust; sprinkle with mozzarella cheese. Arrange cheese nuggets, ends touching, in circle 1 inch from edge of crust. Arrange chicken, olives and bell pepper inside circle of cheese nuggets; sprinkle with Parmesan cheese.
3. Bake 12 to 15 minutes or until nuggets are golden brown and edge of crust is deep golden brown.

1 SERVING: Calories 355 (Calories from Fat 155); Fat 17g (Saturated 7g); Cholesterol 65mg; Sodium 630mg; Carbohydrate 25g (Dietary Fiber 1g); Protein 27g • % Daily Value: Vitamin A 18%; Vitamin C 14%; Calcium 38%; Iron 12% • Exchanges: 1 1/2 Starch, 1 Vegetable, 3 Medium-Fat Meat • Carbohydrate Choices: 1 1/2

together time

Make learning fun. Fill two glasses with water. Add an older egg to one, a fresh-from-the-store egg to the other. Eggs-actly which one floats?

Easy Mexican Chicken and Beans

4 SERVINGS   PREP: 8 MIN   COOK: 20 MIN

1 pound boneless, skinless chicken breast strips for stir-fry

1 envelope (1 1/4 ounces) taco seasoning mix

1 can (15 to 16 ounces) pinto or black beans, rinsed and drained

1 can (11 ounces) whole kernel corn with red and green peppers, undrained

1/4 cup water

Tortillas, if desired

1. Spray 10-inch nonstick skillet with cooking spray; heat over medium-high heat. Cook chicken in skillet 8 to 10 minutes, stirring occasionally, until no longer pink in center.
2. Stir in seasoning mix, beans, corn and water. Cook over medium-high heat 8 to 10 minutes, stirring frequently, until sauce is slightly thickened. Serve with tortillas.

1 SERVING: Calories 320 (Calories from Fat 45); Fat 5g (Saturated 1g); Cholesterol 70mg; Sodium 780mg; Carbohydrate 48g (Dietary Fiber 12g); Protein 36g • % Daily Value: Vitamin A 18%; Vitamin C 12%; Calcium 8%; Iron 24% • Exchanges: 3 Starch, 3 Very Lean Meat • Carbohydrate Choices: 3

together time

Explore other countries. While eating Mexican food, you can talk about Mexican holidays and customs. Get a book about Mexico for ideas. Then talk about starting a family fiesta of your own!

Southwest Chicken Skillet

4 SERVINGS PREP: 5 MIN COOK: 20 MIN

1 tablespoon vegetable oil

1 pound boneless, skinless chicken breasts, cut into 1-inch pieces

1 bag (1 pound) frozen broccoli, corn and red peppers

1 can (15 ounces) black beans, rinsed and drained

1 cup thick-and-chunky salsa

2 cups coarsely crushed tortilla chips

1 cup shredded Cheddar cheese (4 ounces)

1. Heat oil in 10-inch skillet over medium-high heat. Cook chicken in oil 4 to 5 minutes, stirring occasionally, until brown.
2. Stir in frozen vegetables, beans and salsa; reduce heat to medium. Cover and cook 6 to 8 minutes, stirring occasionally, until vegetables are crisp-tender.
3. Sprinkle with tortilla chips and cheese. Cover and cook about 2 minutes or until cheese is melted.

1 SERVING: Calories 645 (Calories from Fat 235); Fat 26g (Saturated 9g); Cholesterol 100mg; Sodium 1180mg; Carbohydrate 67g (Dietary Fiber 13g); Protein 48g • % Daily Value: Vitamin A 68%; Vitamin C 70%; Calcium 30%; Iron 34% • Exchanges: 4 Starch, 1 Vegetable, 5 Lean Meat, 1/2 Fat • Carbohydrate Choices: 4 1/2

together time

Let the kids roll along with dinner preparation. In this recipe, crush the tortilla chips neatly and easily by placing them in a heavy-duty plastic food-storage bag and rolling them with a rolling pin.

Southwest Chicken Skillet

Easy Fish and Veggie Packets

4 PACKETS   PREP: 10 MIN   BAKE: 20 MIN

4 mild-flavored fish fillets, such as cod, flounder, sole or walleye pike (about 4 ounces each)

1 bag (1 pound) frozen broccoli, cauliflower and carrots (or other combination), thawed and drained

1 tablespoon chopped fresh or 1 teaspoon dried dill weed

1/2 teaspoon salt

1/4 teaspoon pepper

1/4 cup dry white wine or chicken broth

1. Heat oven to 450°. Place each fish fillet on 12-inch square of aluminum foil. Top each fish fillet with one-fourth of the vegetables. Sprinkle with dill weed, salt and pepper. Drizzle 1 tablespoon wine over each mound of vegetables.
2. Fold foil over fish and vegetables so edges meet. Seal edges, making tight 1/2-inch fold; fold again. Allow space on sides for circulation and expansion. Place packets on ungreased cookie sheet.
3. Bake about 20 minutes or until vegetables are crisp-tender and fish flakes easily with fork. Place packets on plates. Cut large × across top of each packet; fold back foil.

1 PACKET: Calories 130 (Calories from Fat 20); Fat 2g (Saturated 0g); Cholesterol 60mg; Sodium 420mg; Carbohydrate 6g (Dietary Fiber 3g); Protein 24g • % Daily Value: Vitamin A 62%; Vitamin C 30%; Calcium 6%; Iron 4% • Exchanges: 3 Very Lean Meat, 1 Vegetable • Carbohydrate Choices: 1/2

together time

Color a tablecloth. Cover your table with brown paper or butcher paper, get out the crayons or markers and let the kids draw their neighborhood, complete with your house, yard, school, pets, friends, streets and other buildings or things they notice.

Pasta and Bean Skillet

4 SERVINGS   PREP: 10 MIN   COOK: 15 MIN

1 cup salsa

2/3 cup uncooked elbow macaroni, wagon wheel pasta or small pasta shells (2 ounces)

3/4 cup water

2 teaspoons chili powder

1 can (15 to 16 ounces) pork and beans, undrained, or kidney beans, rinsed and drained

1 can (8 ounces) tomato sauce

1/2 cup shredded Cheddar cheese (2 ounces)

1. Heat all ingredients except cheese to boiling in 10-inch nonstick skillet; reduce heat to low.
2. Cover and simmer about 15 minutes, stirring frequently, just until macaroni is tender. Sprinkle with cheese.

1 SERVING: Calories 280 (Calories from Fat 65); Fat 7g (Saturated 4g); Cholesterol 20mg; Sodium 1220mg; Carbohydrate 41g (Dietary Fiber 8g); Protein 13g • % Daily Value: Vitamin A 48%; Vitamin C 16%; Calcium 16%; Iron 30% • Exchanges: 2 Starch, 2 Vegetable, 1/2 Medium-Fat Meat, 1 Fat • Carbohydrate Choices: 3

together time

Use it up! Make dinner fun by using different pasta shapes and colors, and let the kids add it to the pot. You'll also use up those half-empty boxes in the cupboard. Start with the pasta that takes the longest time to cook, then add faster-cooking pasta.

Chapter 2

Breakfast Dinners with Love

Tasty pancakes with ham and apples? Cinnamon French toast sticks dipped in syrup? Pizza topped with eggs and sausage? Hey, wait a minute! Is this breakfast or dinner? As long as it's quick to fix, everyone likes it and it's a wholesome meal, what difference does it make? Kids and adults alike love pancakes, waffles and eggs, so how about a little breakfast for dinner?

Egg Salad Buns (page 42)

Egg Salad Buns

Photo on page 41

4 SERVINGS PREP: 10 MIN

6 hard-cooked eggs, peeled and finely chopped

1/2 cup diced celery

3 tablespoons pickle relish

3 tablespoons reduced-fat mayonnaise

12 mini sandwich buns, split

3/4 cup canned shoestring potatoes

1. Mix all ingredients except buns and shoestring potatoes in medium bowl.
2. Spread egg salad mixture on bottom halves of buns. Sprinkle with potatoes. Cover with top halves of buns. Wrap in plastic wrap; refrigerate to grab and go.

3 BUNS: Calories 435 (Calories from Fat 165); Fat 18g (Saturated 4g); Cholesterol 322mg; Sodium 705mg; Carbohydrate 48g (Dietary Fiber 3g); Protein 16g • % Daily Value: Vitamin A 9%; Vitamin C 6%; Calcium 15%; Iron 18% • Exchanges: 3 Starch, 1 1/2 Medium-Fat Meat, 1 1/2 Fat • Carbohydrate Choices: 3

together time

Add a little magic by making magic licorice wands with the kids' help. Dip the ends of licorice twists in melted candy coating, then quickly scatter on candy sprinkles. Shazaam! They're done—just let cool 20 minutes before eating.

Breakfast Calzones

4 CALZONES PREP: 5 MIN COOK: 5 MIN BAKE: 13 MIN

4 eggs

1/4 cup milk

2 teaspoons butter or margarine

1 can (10 ounces) refrigerated pizza crust dough

1/2 cup shredded mozzarella cheese (2 ounces)

16 slices (about 3 ounces) pepperoni

4 teaspoons grated Parmesan cheese

1. Heat oven to 400°. Spray large cookie sheet with cooking spray. Beat eggs and milk in medium bowl with fork or wire whisk until well blended. Melt butter in 10-inch nonstick skillet over medium heat. Add egg mixture to skillet. Cook 3 to 5 minutes, stirring occasionally, until eggs are set but moist.
2. Unroll pizza crust dough; pat into 14 × 10-inch rectangle. Cut dough into four 7 × 5-inch rectangles. Divide mozzarella cheese evenly onto half of each rectangle to within 1/2 inch of edges. Top cheese with pepperoni, Parmesan cheese and eggs. Fold dough over filling; press edges firmly to seal. Place on cookie sheet.
3. Bake 11 to 13 minutes or until golden brown.

1 CALZONE: **Calories 445 (Calories from Fat 215); Fat 24g (Saturated 9g); Cholesterol 240mg; Sodium 960mg; Carbohydrate 37g (Dietary Fiber 1g); Protein 21g • % Daily Value: Vitamin A 10%; Vitamin C 0%; Calcium 18%; Iron 18% • Exchanges: 2 1/2 Starch, 2 Medium-Fat Meat • Carbohydrate Choices: 2 1/2**

together time

Make pretty place mats. Pick fallen leaves from your yard in the fall. Place the leaves under mat-sized paper, then rub the flat side of a crayon over the paper and leaves.

Breakfast Burritos

4 BURRITOS PREP: 10 MIN COOK: 10 MIN

1 tablespoon butter or margarine

4 medium green onions, sliced (1/4 cup)

1 1/2 medium green, red or yellow bell peppers, chopped (1 1/2 cups)

6 eggs

2 tablespoons milk

1/2 teaspoon salt

1/4 teaspoon pepper

4 flour tortillas (7 or 8 inches in diameter), heated

1/2 cup shredded Monterey Jack cheese with jalapeño peppers (2 ounces)

1. Melt butter in 10-inch nonstick skillet over medium-high heat. Cook onions and bell peppers in butter 2 to 3 minutes, stirring occasionally, until crisp-tender.
2. Beat eggs, milk, salt and pepper in medium bowl with fork or wire whisk until well mixed. Pour egg mixture over vegetables in skillet. Reduce heat to medium. Cook 4 to 6 minutes, stirring frequently, until eggs are set but still moist.
3. Spoon egg mixture onto warm tortillas; sprinkle with cheese. Roll up tortillas.

1 BURRITO: Calories 320 (Calories from Fat 160); Fat 18g (Saturated 8g); Cholesterol 340mg; Sodium 640mg; Carbohydrate 23g (Dietary Fiber 2g); Protein 17g • % Daily Value: Vitamin A 34%; Vitamin C 58%; Calcium 20%; Iron 12% • Exchanges: 1 1/2 Starch, 1 Medium-Fat Meat, 3 Fat • Carbohydrate Choices: 1 1/2

together time

Pretend your kitchen's a cafeteria. Have everyone stop at the "window" (your counter), order their food and pick it up (on a plate). Another family member can have the drinks already on the table.

Breakfast Burritos

Ham and Swiss Pizza

6 SLICES PREP: 10 MIN COOK: 5 MIN BAKE: 10 MIN

6 large eggs, beaten

1 package (10 ounces) ready-to-serve thin Italian pizza crust (10 inches in diameter)

1/4 cup mayonnaise or salad dressing

2 tablespoons Dijon mustard

1/2 cup diced fully cooked ham

4 medium green onions, sliced (1/4 cup)

1/4 cup chopped red bell pepper

1 cup shredded Swiss cheese (4 ounces)

1. Heat oven to 400°. Spray 10-inch nonstick skillet with cooking spray; heat over medium heat. Pour eggs into skillet. As eggs begin to set at bottom and side, gently lift cooked portions with spatula so that thin, uncooked portion can flow to bottom. Avoid constant stirring. Cook 4 to 5 minutes or until eggs are thickened throughout but still moist.
2. Place pizza crust on ungreased cookie sheet. Mix mayonnaise and mustard; spread evenly over crust. Top with eggs, ham, onions, bell pepper and cheese.
3. Bake about 10 minutes or until cheese is melted.

1 SLICE: Calories 370 (Calories from Fat 200); Fat 22g (Saturated 7g); Cholesterol 240mg; Sodium 680mg; Carbohydrate 26g (Dietary Fiber 1g); Protein 18g • % Daily Value: Vitamin A 18%; Vitamin C 10%; Calcium 22%; Iron 14% • Exchanges: 1 1/2 Starch, 2 High-Fat Meat, 1 Fat • Carbohydrate Choices: 2

together time

Use the creative side of everyone's brains by building a story together during dinner. Start by describing a character, then let each person take turns adding to the story.

Sausage and Egg Breakfast Pizza

6 SLICES PREP: 5 MIN COOK: 5 MIN BAKE: 12 MIN

1 package (8 ounces) frozen brown-and-serve pork sausage links, cut into 1/2-inch pieces

6 eggs, beaten

2 packages (8 ounces each) ready-to-serve Italian pizza crusts or 4 pita breads (6 inches in diameter)

1 1/2 cups shredded Cheddar cheese (6 ounces)

1. Heat oven to 400°. Spray 10-inch nonstick skillet with cooking spray; heat over medium heat. Cook sausage in skillet about 3 minutes, stirring occasionally, until brown. Remove sausage from skillet; drain and set aside. Wipe out skillet with paper towels.
2. Pour eggs into same skillet. As eggs begin to set at bottom and side, gently lift cooked portions with spatula so that thin, uncooked portion can flow to bottom. Avoid constant stirring. Cook 4 to 5 minutes or until eggs are thickened throughout but still moist.
3. Place pizza crusts on ungreased cookie sheet. Sprinkle with half of the cheese. Top with eggs and sausage. Sprinkle with remaining cheese. Bake 10 to 12 minutes or until cheese is melted.

1 1/2 SLICES: Calories 455 (Calories from Fat 205); Fat 23g (Saturated 10g); Cholesterol 260mg; Sodium 910mg; Carbohydrate 39g (Dietary Fiber 2g); Protein 23g • % Daily Value: Vitamin A 12%; Vitamin C 0%; Calcium 24%; Iron 18% • Exchanges: 2 1/2 Starch, 2 High-Fat Meat, 1 Fat • Carbohydrate Choices: 2 1/2

together time

Declare a pizza night! For dessert, bake a brownie mix in a pizza pan. The family can decorate it with a tub of frosting and candies.

family fun

MEXICAN NIGHT

For a fun family fiesta, there's so much more than nachos and tacos. Follow these sunny menu ideas to add some "olé" to everyday. Or choose from the many other favorite Mexican main dishes in this cookbook—to bring extra sparkle to dinner with the tropical flavors of cilantro, chiles, lime and salsa.

Menu

Mexi Snack Mix (at right)

Double-Wrapped Turkey Tacos (page 86)

Nacho Celery (at right) or sliced red bell peppers

Cinnamon "Fried" Ice Cream (at right)

Corbis Digital Stock

Mexi Snack Mix

Mix 3 cups **bite-size cheese crackers**, 2 cups **pretzel twists** and 1 cup **salted peanuts** in 2 1/2-quart microwavable bowl. Drizzle with 1 tablespoon **vegetable oil**; toss to coat. Sprinkle with 2 tablespoons **taco seasoning mix** (from 1 1/4-ounce envelope); toss to coat. Microwave uncovered on High 2 minutes; stir. Microwave 2 minutes longer. Spread on waxed paper; cool 5 minutes before serving.

Nacho Celery

Mix 1 cup **smoke-flavored cold-pack cheese spread** and 1 teaspoon **taco seasoning mix** (from 1 1/4-ounce envelope) in small bowl. Spread mixture in four 10-inch **celery stalks**. Cut into 2-inch sections.

Cinnamon "Fried" Ice Cream

Crush 3 cups **Cinnamon Toast Crunch® cereal**; place in shallow pan. Quickly roll 6 scoops (1/2 cup each) **vanilla ice cream** (1 scoop at a time) in cereal to coat. Place coated scoops of ice cream in ungreased 15 × 10 × 1-inch baking pan. Cover and freeze about 2 hours. Set oven control to broil. Uncover pan. Broil scoops with tops 6 inches from heat about 30 seconds or until coating is light brown.

More Mexican Ideas

Tired of tacos tonight? Try these other Mexican dishes instead.

Easy Mexican Chicken and Beans (page 35)
Mexican Egg Scramble (page 56)
Mexican Pork (page 124)

helping is fun

Mom or Dad

- Makes filling for celery
- Cooks turkey for tacos
- Scoops ice cream

The Kids

- Measure and microwave snack mix
- Spread filling in celery
- Crush cereal and roll ice cream balls to coat

together time

"Fry" dessert under the broiler after dinner. Earlier in the day, scoop ice cream, roll in crushed crumbs and freeze for at least 2 hours so dessert's ready to go.

Play up the colorful festivity of Mexico by setting the table with multicolored bowls for chips and dip and using bright decorated paper napkins. The kids can make cut-out paper banners to drape around the kitchen.

Read a Mexican storybook about life in Mexico or in the United States for someone who comes from Mexico. Some great choices for all ages include *Hair/Pelitos* by Sandra Cisneros and *Going Home* by Eve Bunting. You might even learn some Spanish words and phrases together.

Accompany dinner with new tunes. Investigate different styles of music, borrow CDs from the library or find tapes of Mexican songs.

Canadian Bacon–Pineapple Sandwiches

4 SANDWICHES PREP: 5 MIN COOK: 5 MIN BROIL: 4 MIN

- 4 canned pineapple slices, well drained
- 4 slices Canadian-style bacon
- 4 English muffins, split
- 3 tablespoons butter or margarine
- 4 hard-cooked eggs, peeled and sliced
- 1/2 cup shredded Colby-Monterey Jack cheese (2 ounces)

1. Cook pineapple slices and Canadian bacon in 10-inch skillet over medium heat 5 minutes, turning once, until thoroughly heated and lightly browned.
2. Meanwhile, toast English muffin halves; spread with butter. Place 4 halves on small ungreased cookie sheet. Place 1 pineapple slice and 1 Canadian bacon slice on each toasted muffin half. Top with egg slices and cheese.
3. Broil with tops 4 to 6 inches from heat 3 to 4 minutes or until cheese is bubbly and sandwiches are thoroughly heated. Top with remaining muffin halves.

1 SANDWICH: Calories 410 (Calories from Fat 190); Fat 21g (Saturated Fat 7g); Cholesterol 240mg; Sodium 840mg; Carbohydrate 35g (Dietary Fiber 2g); Protein 20g • % Daily Value: Vitamin A 18%; Vitamin C 62%; Calcium 24%; Iron 12% • Exchanges: 2 Starch, 1/2 Fruit, 2 Lean Meat, 3 Fat • Carbohydrate Choices: 2

together time

Rake leaves in your yard together before the weather gets too cold. Once the leaves are in a pile, take turns jumping in before bagging them.

Denver Scrambled Egg Mini Pizzas

4 PIZZAS PREP: 5 MIN BAKE: 15 MIN COOK: 10 MIN

1 can (10 ounces) refrigerated pizza crust dough

1 tablespoon butter or margarine

1 cup frozen stir-fry bell peppers and onions (from 1-pound bag)

8 eggs

2 tablespoons milk

1/2 cup chopped fully cooked ham

2 tablespoons creamy mustard-mayonnaise sauce

1. Heat oven to 400°. Lightly spray large cookie sheet with cooking spray. Unroll dough. Cut dough into 4 equal pieces; place on cookie sheet. Press out each piece of dough to form 6 × 5-inch rectangle; form slight rim on edges of rectangles. Bake 11 to 15 minutes or until golden brown.
2. Meanwhile, melt butter in 10-inch nonstick skillet over medium heat. Cook stir-fry vegetables in butter 3 to 5 minutes, stirring occasionally, until tender.
3. Beat eggs, milk and ham in medium bowl with fork or wire whisk until well mixed; stir into vegetables. Cook 4 to 5 minutes, stirring occasionally, until thoroughly cooked and eggs are set but still moist.
4. Spread mustard-mayonnaise sauce on baked crusts. Spoon egg mixture evenly over sauce. Serve warm.

1 PIZZA: Calories 440 (Calories from Fat 200); Total Fat 22g (Saturated Fat 7g); Cholesterol 445mg; Sodium 800mg; Carbohydrate 39g (Dietary Fiber 2g); Protein 22g • % Daily Value: Vitamin A 16%; Vitamin C 14%; Calcium 8%; Iron 20% • Exchanges: 2 1/2 Starch, 2 Medium-Fat Meat, 2 Fat • Carbohydrate Choices: 2 1/2

together time

Schedule a meal with grandparents. Make sure it's a time when no one has to rush off somewhere so the kids can spend some leisurely time with grandparents, a favorite aunt or uncle, or a senior neighbor.

Italian Garden Frittata

4 WEDGES PREP: 5 MIN COOK: 5 MIN BROIL: 3 MIN

8 eggs

1 tablespoon coarsely chopped fresh sage leaves

1/2 teaspoon salt

1/4 teaspoon pepper

1/2 cup grated Parmesan or Romano cheese

1 teaspoon olive or vegetable oil

1 small zucchini, sliced

2 medium green onions, sliced (2 tablespoons)

2 roma (plum) tomatoes, cut lengthwise into thin slices

1. Beat eggs, sage, salt, pepper and 1/4 cup of the cheese in medium bowl with fork or wire whisk until well blended; set aside.
2. Heat oil in 10-inch ovenproof nonstick skillet over medium heat. Add zucchini and onions; cook and stir about 2 minutes or until zucchini is tender. Add egg mixture; cook about 2 minutes, lifting edges occasionally to allow uncooked egg mixture to flow to bottom of skillet, until egg mixture is almost set.
3. Top frittata with tomato slices; sprinkle with remaining 1/4 cup cheese. Set oven control to broil. Broil with top 4 to 6 inches from heat 1 to 3 minutes or until top is set and begins to brown.

1 WEDGE: Calories 230 (Calories from Fat 145); Fat 16g (Saturated 6g); Cholesterol 430mg; Sodium 650mg; Carbohydrate 4g (Dietary Fiber 1g); Protein 18g • % Daily Value: Vitamin A 22%; Vitamin C 6%; Calcium 22%; Iron 8% • Exchanges: 1 Vegetable, 2 Medium-Fat Meat, 1 Fat • Carbohydrate Choices: 0

together time

Make music. Fill glass dinner glasses with different amounts of water. Using a pencil or wooden spoon, carefully tap each glass so the kids can hear how the sounds differ. Let them take turns carefully tapping their glasses to make their own music.

Italian Garden Frittata

Hash Brown Frittata

4 WEDGES PREP: 10 MIN COOK: 25 MIN

2 cups refrigerated shredded hash brown potatoes

1 can (11 ounces) whole kernel corn with red and green peppers, drained

1 teaspoon onion salt

4 eggs

1/4 cup milk

1 1/2 teaspoons chopped fresh or 1/2 teaspoon dried marjoram leaves

1/2 teaspoon red pepper sauce

1/3 cup shredded Cheddar cheese

1. Mix potatoes, corn and onion salt in medium bowl. Spray 10-inch nonstick skillet with cooking spray; heat over medium heat. Pack potato mixture firmly into skillet, leaving 1/2-inch space around edge. Reduce heat to medium-low. Cook uncovered about 10 minutes or until bottom starts to brown.

2. While potato mixture is cooking, beat eggs, milk, marjoram and pepper sauce in medium bowl with fork or wire whisk until well blended. Pour egg mixture over potato mixture. Cook uncovered over medium-low heat. As mixture begins to set on bottom and side, gently lift cooked portions with spatula so that thin, uncooked portion can flow to bottom. Avoid constant stirring. Cook about 5 minutes or until eggs are thickened throughout but still moist.

3. Sprinkle with cheese. Reduce heat to low. Cover and cook about 10 minutes or until center is set and cheese is bubbly. Loosen bottom of frittata with spatula. Cut frittata into 4 wedges.

1 WEDGE: Calories 410 (Calories from Fat 180); Fat 20g (Saturated 7g); Cholesterol 225mg; Sodium 1020mg; Carbohydrate 43g (Dietary Fiber 4g); Protein 14g • % Daily Value: Vitamin A 12%; Vitamin C 14%; Calcium 10%; Iron 8% • Exchanges: 3 Starch, 1 Medium-Fat Meat, 2 Fat • Carbohydrate Choices: 3

together time

Make it fun! Dusting strawberries with powdered sugar looks like a sprinkling of snow on a mountaintop. Dunking carrots into dip is like diving into a creamy pool. Let imaginations soar while bodies get the proper nourishment.

Country Eggs in Tortilla Cups

4 TORTILLA CUPS PREP: 10 MIN BAKE: 10 MIN COOK: 10 MIN

4 flour tortillas (6 inches in diameter)

Cooking spray

2 cups frozen Southern-style hash brown potatoes

1/4 cup chopped green bell pepper

3 eggs

1/4 cup milk

1/4 teaspoon salt

3/4 cup shredded Cheddar cheese (3 ounces)

1/4 cup sour cream

Salsa, if desired

1. Heat oven to 400°. Turn four 6-ounce custard cups upside down onto cookie sheet. Spray both sides of each tortilla lightly with cooking spray. Place tortilla over each cup, gently pressing edges toward cup. Bake 8 to 10 minutes or until light golden brown. Remove tortillas from cups; place upright on serving plates.
2. Spray 8- or 10-inch nonstick skillet with cooking spray; heat over medium heat. Cook potatoes and bell pepper in skillet about 5 minutes, stirring occasionally, until potatoes are light brown. Beat eggs, milk and salt in small bowl with fork or wire whisk until well mixed; stir into potatoes. Cook about 3 minutes, stirring occasionally, until eggs are almost set.
3. Spoon 1/4 of the egg mixture into each tortilla cup. Top with cheese and sour cream. Serve immediately with salsa.

1 TORTILLA CUP: Calories 420 (Calories from Fat 215); Fat 24g (Saturated 10g); Cholesterol 190mg; Sodium 730mg; Carbohydrate 36g (Dietary Fiber 3g); Protein 15g • % Daily Value: Vitamin A 12%; Vitamin C 12%; Calcium 20%; Iron 10% • Exchanges: 2 1/2 Starch, 1 High-Fat Meat, 2 1/2 Fat • Carbohydrate Choices: 2 1/2

together time

Play "I Spy"! Take turns giving three clues for everyone else at the dinner table to guess what you see. It's a great way to sharpen thinking, looking and listening skills.

Mexican Egg Scramble

4 SERVINGS PREP: 10 MIN COOK: 10 MIN

1/4 pound bulk Italian sausage

1/4 cup chopped onion

1/4 cup chopped green or red bell pepper

6 eggs

1/4 cup milk

1 cup shredded Colby-Monterey Jack cheese (4 ounces)

1/4 cup medium or mild salsa

Tortillas, warmed, if desired

1. Cook sausage, onion and bell pepper in 10-inch skillet over medium-high heat, stirring frequently, until sausage is no longer pink; drain.
2. Beat eggs and milk in small bowl with fork. Add to sausage mixture. Reduce heat to medium. Cook about 3 minutes, stirring occasionally, until eggs begin to set. Gently stir in cheese. Continue cooking about 2 minutes, until cheese is melted and eggs are set.
3. Remove from heat. Spoon salsa over egg mixture. Serve immediately with additional salsa and tortillas.

1 SERVING: Calories 315 (Calories from Fat 210); Fat 23g (Saturated 10g); Cholesterol 360mg; Sodium 490mg; Carbohydrate 5g (Dietary Fiber 1g); Protein 21g • % Daily Value: Vitamin A 28%; Vitamin C 16%; Calcium 26%; Iron 8% • Exchanges: 3 Medium-Fat Meat, 2 Fat • Carbohydrate Choices: 0

together time

Learn to zap. With adult supervision, have the kids pop a bag of microwave popcorn and munch away while you watch your favorite movie. If you're up to it, make Puffy Popcorn Balls (page 135).

Chili-Cheese Hash Browns

4 SERVINGS PREP: 5 MIN COOK: 10 MIN

1 package (12 ounces) frozen chili

4 frozen rectangular hash-brown potato patties (from 27-ounce package)

Vegetable oil

1/2 cup finely shredded Cheddar cheese (2 ounces)

1/2 cup thick-and-chunky salsa

1 tablespoon chopped fresh cilantro, if desired

1. Heat chili as directed on package. Fry potato patties in oil as directed on package.
2. Arrange potato patties on individual serving plates. Top each serving with chili. Sprinkle with cheese. Top with salsa and cilantro.

1 SERVING: Calories 615 (Calories from Fat 260); Fat 29g (Saturated 9g); Cholesterol 25mg; Sodium 1270mg; Carbohydrate 58g (Dietary Fiber 7g); Protein 13g • % Daily Value: Vitamin A 14%; Vitamin C 20%; Calcium 12%; Iron 14% • Exchanges: 4 Starch, 6 Fat • Carbohydrate Choices: 4

together time

Enjoy a nostalgia game night. Pick a favorite childhood game—jacks, marbles or Chinese checkers—and play it together. Other fun games to try: Clue, Monopoly or Twister for more of a workout.

Tostada Waffles

10 WAFFLES PREP: 10 MIN BAKE: 20 MIN

2 cups Original Bisquick® mix

1 1/3 cups milk

2 tablespoons vegetable oil

1 egg

1 can (4 1/2 ounces) chopped green chiles, drained

1 teaspoon chili powder

1 pound ground beef

1 envelope (1 1/4 ounces) taco seasoning mix

6 cups shredded lettuce

1 cup shredded Cheddar cheese (4 ounces)

2 medium tomatoes, chopped (1 1/2 cups)

1 1/2 cups sour cream

2 medium green onions, sliced (2 tablespoons)

1. Heat waffle iron; grease with vegetable oil if necessary (or spray with cooking spray before heating). Stir Bisquick mix, milk, oil and egg in large bowl until blended. Stir in chiles and chili powder.

2. Pour batter from cup or pitcher onto center of hot waffle iron. (Waffle irons vary in size; check manufacturer's directions for recommended amount of batter.) Close lid of waffle iron. Bake until steaming stops and waffle is golden brown. Carefully remove waffle. Repeat with remaining batter.

3. Cook beef as directed on envelope of taco seasoning mix. Top waffles with beef and remaining ingredients.

1 WAFFLE: Calories 370 (Calories from Fat 215); Fat 24g (Saturated 11g); Cholesterol 85mg; Sodium 660mg; Carbohydrate 23g (Dietary Fiber 1g); Protein 16g • % Daily Value: Vitamin A 22%; Vitamin C 10%; Calcium 20%; Iron 12% • Exchanges: 1 1/2 Starch, 2 High-Fat Meat, 1 Fat • Carbohydrate Choices: 1 1/2

together time

Construct a tostada! Set out all the ingredients, including shredded lettuce, shredded cheese, chopped tomatoes, sliced green onions, sour cream and salsa, and let everyone "build" his or her own dinner.

Tostada Waffles

Ham and Mozzarella Brunch Bake

8 SERVINGS PREP: 15 MIN BAKE: 45 MIN STAND: 5 MIN

6 eggs

1 container (12 ounces) small curd creamed cottage cheese

1/2 cup all-purpose flour

1 teaspoon baking powder

2 teaspoons yellow mustard

1/4 teaspoon pepper

2 cups finely chopped fully cooked ham

2 cups shredded mozzarella cheese (8 ounces)

1/2 cup chive-and-onion soft cream cheese (from 8-ounce tub)

1. Heat oven to 350°. Spray rectangular baking dish, 13 × 9 × 2 inches, with cooking spray.
2. Beat eggs in large bowl with fork. Stir in cottage cheese. Stir in remaining ingredients except cream cheese. Drop cream cheese by 1/2 teaspoonfuls into egg mixture; fold in. Pour into baking dish.
3. Bake uncovered 40 to 45 minutes or until set in center. Let stand 5 minutes before cutting. Cut into squares.

1 SERVING: Calories 295 (Calories from Fat 155); Fat 17g (Saturated Fat 9g); Cholesterol 210mg; Sodium 870mg; Carbohydrate 9g (Dietary Fiber 0g); Protein 27g • % Daily Value: Vitamin A 12%; Vitamin C 0%; Calcium 30%; Iron 8% • Exchanges: 1/2 Starch, 3 1/2 Medium-Fat Meat • Carbohydrate Choices: 1/2

together time

Design a card. If you have people coming for dinner or brunch, kids can get creative and help by writing the guests' names and drawing designs on folded index or place cards. Have the kids place them above each plate.

Cinnamon French Toast Sticks with Spicy Cider Syrup

10 SERVINGS PREP: 10 MIN COOK: 10 MIN

Spicy Cider Syrup (below)

1/2 cup all-purpose flour

1 1/4 cups milk

2 teaspoons ground cinnamon

1 teaspoon vanilla

2 eggs

10 slices sandwich bread, cut into thirds

Spicy Cider Syrup

1 cup sugar

3 tablespoons all-purpose flour

1/4 teaspoon ground cinnamon

1/4 teaspoon ground nutmeg

2 cups apple cider

2 tablespoons lemon juice

1/4 cup butter or margarine

1. Make Spicy Cider Syrup; keep warm. Spray griddle or skillet with cooking spray; heat griddle to 375° or heat skillet over medium heat.
2. Beat remaining ingredients except bread in small bowl with fork until smooth. Dip sticks of bread into batter; drain excess batter back into bowl.
3. Place bread on griddle. Cook about 4 minutes on each side or until golden brown. Serve with syrup.

Spicy Cider Syrup

Mix sugar, flour, cinnamon and nutmeg in 2-quart saucepan. Stir in cider and lemon juice. Cook over medium heat, stirring constantly, until mixture thickens and boils. Boil and stir 1 minute; remove from heat. Stir in butter.

1 SERVING: Calories 265 (Calories from Fat 65); Fat 7g (Saturated 4g); Cholesterol 60mg; Sodium 200mg; Carbohydrate 46g (Dietary Fiber 1g); Protein 5g • % Daily Value: Vitamin A 6%; Vitamin C 0%; Calcium 8%; Iron 8% • Exchanges: 2 Starch, 1 Fruit, 1 Fat • Carbohydrate Choices: 3

together time

Take reservations! The kids will have a great time pretending they're the servers at a restaurant. They can print the menu, seat you, take your order and serve dinner. It's fun for them and a great break for the grown-ups.

Stuffed French Toast

12 SLICES   PREP: 15 MIN   COOK: 6 MIN

12 slices French bread, 1/2 inch thick

6 tablespoons soft cream cheese

1/4 cup preserves or jam (any flavor)

2 eggs, 4 egg whites or 1/2 cup fat-free cholesterol-free egg product, slightly beaten

1/2 cup fat-free (skim) milk

2 tablespoons sugar

1. Spread one side of 6 slices bread with 1 tablespoon of the cream cheese. Spread one side of remaining slices with 2 teaspoons of the preserves. Make 6 cream cheese and jelly sandwiches.
2. Beat eggs, milk and sugar with a fork or wire whisk until smooth; pour into shallow bowl.
3. Spray griddle or skillet with cooking spray; heat griddle to 325° or heat skillet over medium-low heat. Dip sandwiches into egg mixture. Cook sandwiches 2 to 3 minutes on each side or until golden brown.

2 SLICES: Calories 460 (Calories from Fat 90); Fat 10g (Saturated 4g); Cholesterol 80mg; Sodium 810mg; Carbohydrate 78g (Dietary Fiber 4g); Protein 15g • % Daily Value: Vitamin A 6%; Vitamin C 0%; Calcium 14%; Iron 22% • Exchanges: 5 Starch, 1 1/2 Fat • Carbohydrate Choices: 5

together time

Name that tune. Get into the groove! During dinner or cleanup, take turns humming or singing a few words or a line from a song and letting other family members guess what the song is.

Italian Pancake Dunkers

8 SERVINGS PREP: 10 MIN COOK: 13 MIN

1 cup pizza or spaghetti sauce

2 cups Original Bisquick mix

1 cup milk

2 eggs

1/2 cup shredded mozzarella cheese (2 ounces)

1/2 cup finely chopped pepperoni

1/4 cup finely chopped green bell pepper

2 teaspoons Italian seasoning

1 small tomato, finely chopped (1/2 cup)

1. Heat pizza sauce until warm; keep warm. Spray griddle or 10-inch nonstick skillet with cooking spray; heat griddle to 375° or heat skillet over medium heat.
2. Stir Bisquick mix, milk and eggs in large bowl until blended. Stir in remaining ingredients. Spoon batter by tablespoonfuls onto hot griddle; spread slightly.
3. Cook pancakes until dry around edges. Turn; cook other sides until golden. To serve, dunk pancakes into pizza sauce.

1 SERVING: Calories 225 (Calories from Fat 100); Fat 10g (Saturated 5g); Cholesterol 75mg; Sodium 800mg; Carbohydrate 25g (Dietary Fiber 0g); Protein 10g • % Daily Value: Vitamin A 10%; Vitamin C 10%; Calcium 10%; Iron 10% • Exchanges: 2 1/2 Starch • Carbohydrate Choices: 1 1/2

together time

Spare some change. Kids love tiny pancakes for their small size. Silver dollar pancakes can spark a discussion about the silver dollar coin and other types of coins.

Italian Pancake Dunkers

Oatmeal Pancakes with Maple-Cranberry Syrup

6 SERVINGS   PREP: 10 MIN   COOK: 15 MIN

Maple-Cranberry Syrup (below)

1/2 cup quick-cooking or old-fashioned oats

1/4 cup all-purpose flour

1/4 cup whole wheat flour

3/4 cup buttermilk

1/4 cup fat-free (skim) milk

1 tablespoon sugar

2 tablespoons vegetable oil

1 teaspoon baking powder

1/2 teaspoon baking soda

1/2 teaspoon salt

1 egg

Maple-Cranberry Syrup

1/2 cup maple-flavored syrup

1/4 cup whole berry cranberry sauce

1. Make Maple-Cranberry Syrup; keep warm. Beat remaining ingredients in medium bowl with hand beater or wire whisk just until smooth. (For thinner pancakes, stir in additional 2 to 4 tablespoons milk.)
2. Spray griddle or 10-inch nonstick skillet with cooking spray; heat griddle to 375° or heat skillet over medium heat. For each pancake, pour slightly less than 1/4 cup batter from cup or pitcher onto hot griddle.
3. Cook pancakes until puffed and dry around edges. Turn; cook other sides until golden brown. Serve with syrup.

Maple-Cranberry Syrup

Heat ingredients in 1-quart saucepan over medium heat, stirring occasionally, until cranberry sauce is melted.

1 SERVING: Calories 250 (Calories from Fat 65); Fat 7g (Saturated 1g); Cholesterol 40mg; Sodium 400mg; Carbohydrate 41g (Dietary Fiber 2g); Protein 5g • % Daily Value: Vitamin A 2%; Vitamin C 0%; Calcium 12%; Iron 6% • Exchanges: 2 Starch, 1/2 Fruit, 1/2 Other Carbohydrate, 1 1/2 Fat • Carbohydrate Choices: 3

together time

Make happy fruit faces for dessert. On dessert plates, arrange blueberries and peach and plum slices to make eyes, nose, mouth and ears. Kids will gobble it up!

Ham and Apple Pancakes

6 SERVINGS PREP: 5 MIN COOK: 15 MIN

1 can (21 ounces) apple pie filling

2 cups Original Bisquick mix

1 cup milk

2 eggs

1 1/2 cups diced fully cooked ham

1 cup shredded Cheddar cheese (4 ounces)

Ground cinnamon, if desired

1. Heat pie filling until warm; keep warm. Spray griddle or 10-inch nonstick skillet with cooking spray; heat griddle to 375° or heat skillet over medium heat.
2. Stir Bisquick mix, milk and eggs in large bowl until blended. Fold in ham and cheese. For each pancake, pour slightly less than 1/4 cup batter onto hot griddle.
3. Cook pancakes until dry around edges. Turn; cook other sides until golden brown. Top with pie filling; sprinkle with cinnamon.

1 SERVING: Calories 430 (Calories from Fat 155); Fat 17g (Saturated 7g); Cholesterol 115mg; Sodium 1230mg; Carbohydrate 50g (Dietary Fiber 2g); Protein 19g • % Daily Value: Vitamin A 8%; Vitamin C 0%; Calcium 22%; Iron 12% • Exchanges: 2 Starch, 1 Fruit, 2 Medium-Fat Meat, 1 1/2 Fat • Carbohydrate Choices: 3

together time

Explore your neighborhood. Pair up with the kids and go on a scavenger hunt in your neighborhood. Be the first to find a feather, a dandelion, an oak leaf, a smooth rock, a twig or whatever your neighborhood has to offer.

Chapter 3

Grab 'n Go Dinners

Soccer game night? Dashing off to dance class? When you have so many choices for easy on-the-go dinners, all waiting to be homemade by yours truly in minutes, the temptation to stop by the fast-food joint completely melts away. Your only decision becomes whether you'll have a real picnic in the car or if there's time for a pretend picnic on your living room floor.

Ham and Provolone Rolls (page 70)

Ham and Provolone Rolls

Photo on page 69

4 ROLLS   PREP: 10 MIN

1/4 cup mayonnaise or salad dressing

2 cloves garlic, finely chopped

4 flour tortillas (8 to 10 inches in diameter)

1 cup fresh spinach leaves, stems removed

8 ounces thinly sliced ham

4 ounces thinly sliced provolone cheese

2 medium tomatoes, thinly sliced

1. Mix mayonnaise and garlic; spread evenly over tortillas.
2. Top tortillas with layers of spinach, ham, cheese and tomatoes; roll up tightly. Serve immediately, or wrap securely with plastic wrap and refrigerate up to 24 hours to grab 'n go.

1 ROLL: Calories 425 (Calories from Fat 215); Fat 24g (Saturated 8g); Cholesterol 55mg; Sodium 1010mg; Carbohydrate 30g (Dietary Fiber 2g); Protein 22g • % Daily Value: Vitamin A 28%; Vitamin C 22%; Calcium 20%; Iron 14% • Exchanges: 2 Starch, 2 Medium-Fat Meat, 2 1/2 Fat • Carbohydrate Choices: 2

together time

Have the kids make their own trail mix. They can mix up their individual creations of popcorn, assorted cereals, raisins or other dried fruit, small crackers, chocolate candies and other favorites and snack away.

Beef, Lettuce and Tomato Wraps

4 WRAPS PREP: 20 MIN BROIL: 10 MIN

1 1/2 tablespoons chili powder

2 teaspoons dried oregano leaves

1 teaspoon ground cumin

1 teaspoon salt

1-pound beef top sirloin steak, about 3/4 inch thick

4 flour tortillas (6 to 8 inches in diameter)

3/4 cup reduced-fat sour cream

1 tablespoon prepared horseradish

4 cups shredded lettuce

1 large tomato, chopped (1 cup)

1. Mix chili powder, oregano, cumin and salt. Rub mixture on both sides of beef. Let stand 10 minutes at room temperature.
2. Set oven control to broil. Place beef on rack in broiler pan. Broil with top 3 to 4 inches from heat about 5 minutes on each side for medium doneness or until beef is desired doneness. Cut into 1/8-inch slices.
3. Warm tortillas as directed on package. Mix sour cream and horseradish. Spread 3 tablespoons horseradish mixture over each tortilla; top each with 1 cup of the lettuce and 1/4 cup of the tomato. Top with beef. Wrap tortillas around filling. Serve immediately, or wrap securely with plastic wrap and refrigerate up to 24 hours to grab 'n go.

1 WRAP: Calories 280 (Calories from Fat 80); Fat 9g (Saturated 4g); Cholesterol 75mg; Sodium 840mg; Carbohydrate 25g (Dietary Fiber 3g); Protein 29g • % Daily Value: Vitamin A 36%; Vitamin C 22%; Calcium 12%; Iron 20% • Exchanges: 1 Starch, 2 Vegetable, 3 Lean Meat • Carbohydrate Choices: 1 1/2

together time

Visit your local farmers' market and try different varieties of your favorite fruits or vegetables than the ones you find at the supermarket; have the kids look for heirloom tomatoes, sweet corn or white peaches.

Ranch Beef Pitas

4 PITA HALVES   PREP: 15 MIN

2 pita breads (8 inches in diameter)

4 cups romaine and leaf lettuce (from 10-ounce bag)

1/2 pound cubed cooked roast beef (1 1/3 cups)

4 roma (plum) tomatoes, cut lengthwise in half, then sliced

1/2 cup ranch dressing

1/4 cup sliced red onion, if desired

1. Cut pita breads in half; open to form pockets.
2. Toss lettuce, beef, tomatoes and dressing in large bowl. Divide among pita bread halves. Top with onion. Serve immediately, or wrap securely with plastic wrap and refrigerate up to 24 hours to grab 'n go.

1/2 PITA: Calories 415 (Calories from Fat 205); Fat 23g (Saturated 5g); Cholesterol 55mg; Sodium 580mg; Carbohydrate 31g (Dietary Fiber 3g); Protein 22g • % Daily Value: Vitamin A 32%; Vitamin C 38%; Calcium 10%; Iron 20% • Exchanges: 2 Starch, 2 Medium-Fat Meat, 2 Fat • Carbohydrate Choices: 2

together time

Make it an "eat-in" night! Bag up an individual meal for each family member to "drive through" and pick up. Use paper money and include a math lesson with this happy, fun meal!

Ranch Beef Pitas

Inside-Out Beef Wrap-Ups

4 WRAPS PREP: 10 MIN

2 purchased regular or Italian-flavor soft breadsticks, about 7 × 1 3/4 inches

1/4 cup soft cream cheese with onions and chives (from 8-ounce tub)

4 slices (1 ounce each) process American cheese

4 slices deli roast beef, about 7 × 3 inches

4 large leaf lettuce leaves

8 pretzel sticks

1. Cut each breadstick crosswise in half. Cut each half lengthwise not quite through to bottom of breadstick. Spread 1 tablespoon cream cheese onto one cut side of slit.

2. Center cheese slice on beef slice. Wrap beef and cheese around breadstick, with beef on the outside. Wrap lettuce leaf around beef on breadstick. Secure with pretzel sticks. Serve immediately, or wrap securely with plastic wrap and refrigerate up to 24 hours to grab 'n go.

1 WRAP: Calories 250 (Calories from Fat 135); Fat 15g (Saturated 8g); Cholesterol 55mg; Sodium 580mg; Carbohydrate 13g (Dietary Fiber 1g); Protein 16g • % Daily Value: Vitamin A 10%; Vitamin C 0%; Calcium 16%; Iron 8% • Exchanges: 1 Starch, 2 Medium-Fat Meat, 1/2 Fat • Carbohydrate Choices: 1

together time

Pack a picnic. Place an old shower curtain on the floor, and cover it with a colorful tablecloth. Eat your dinner as a picnic, and enjoy each other's company while munching away. The nice thing? No bugs!

Beef in Pita Pockets

4 PITA HALVES PREP: 15 MIN

2 pita breads (6 inches in diameter)

1/3 cup country-style or creamy Dijon mustard

1/2 pound thinly sliced cooked deli roast beef

1 small tomato, thinly sliced

4 slices (1 ounce each) Cheddar or provolone cheese

4 lettuce leaves

1. Cut pita breads in half; open to form pockets. Spread mustard on inside of pita pocket halves.
2. Fill pockets with beef, tomato, cheese and lettuce. Serve immediately, or wrap securely with plastic wrap and refrigerate up to 24 hours to grab 'n go.

1/2 PITA: Calories 365 (Calories from Fat 115); Fat 13g (Saturated 6g); Cholesterol 70mg; Sodium 1080mg; Carbohydrate 32g (Dietary Fiber 2g); Protein 31g • % Daily Value: Vitamin A 14%; Vitamin C 12%; Calcium 26%; Iron 20% • Exchanges: 2 Starch, 3 1/2 Lean Meat, 1/2 Fat • Carbohydrate Choices: 2

together time

Go fly a kite! What better thing to do on a windy spring day than flying kites? Beginning kite fliers should start with an affordable kite. A kite without a center spine is durable and crash resistant. If a kite is too fast, add a tail so it will be easier to fly.

Pizza Turnovers

4 TURNOVERS   PREP: 12 MIN   BAKE: 15 MIN

1 can (10 ounces) refrigerated pizza crust dough

1/4 cup pizza sauce

1/4 cup finely shredded carrot

24 slices pepperoni (1 to 1 1/4 inches in diameter)

1 tablespoon grated Parmesan cheese

2 slices mozzarella cheese (1 1/2 ounces), cut in half

1. Heat oven to 400°. Roll pizza crust dough on lightly floured surface into 12-inch square. Cut dough into four 6-inch squares.

2. Spread about 1 tablespoon pizza sauce on each square to within 1/2 inch of edges. Top with carrot, pepperoni and cheeses. Fold each square in half over filling; press edges to seal. Place on ungreased cookie sheet.

3. Bake 12 to 15 minutes or until light golden brown. Serve immediately, or wrap securely with plastic wrap and refrigerate up to 24 hours to grab 'n go.

1 TURNOVER: Calories 445 (Calories from Fat 215); Fat 24g (Saturated 9g); Cholesterol 40mg; Sodium 1220mg; Carbohydrate 38g (Dietary Fiber 2g); Protein 19g • % Daily Value: Vitamin A 30%; Vitamin C 2%; Calcium 18%; Iron 16% • Exchanges: 2 1/2 Starch, 1 1/2 High-Fat Meat, 2 Fat • Carbohydrate Choices: 2 1/2

together time

Make easy frozen smoothies. Mix equal parts of vanilla pudding and any flavor of fruited yogurt, pour into small paper cups and freeze for a couple of hours. Place a wooden stick in each partially frozen pop after 30 minutes.

Pizza Turnovers

Pastrami Deli Folds

6 SERVINGS PREP: 15 MIN

- 1 pint (2 cups) deli coleslaw (creamy style)
- 1 tablespoon prepared horseradish
- 1 to 2 teaspoons grated lemon peel
- 1 pound sliced turkey pastrami
- 2 small red bell peppers, cut into 1/4-inch strips
- 1 bag (15 ounces) pita fold breads

1. Mix coleslaw, horseradish and lemon peel in small bowl.
2. Arrange pastrami, coleslaw and bell pepper strips on half of each pita fold bread; fold over. Serve immediately, or wrap securely with plastic wrap and refrigerate up to 24 hours to grab 'n go.

1/2 PITA: Calories 395 (Calories from Fat 125); Fat 14g (Saturated 3g); Cholesterol 45mg; Sodium 1280mg; Carbohydrate 49g (Dietary Fiber 3g); Protein 21g% • Daily Value: Vitamin A 58%; Vitamin C 100%; Calcium 8%; Iron 20% • Exchanges: 3 Starch, 1 1/2 Medium-Fat Meat, 1 Vegetable • Carbohydrate Choices: 3

together time

Cool off the kids with apple juice poured over scoops ("snowballs") of frozen yogurt or sherbet. Serve in paper cups with plastic spoons.

Italian Country Sandwich

6 SANDWICHES PREP: 10 MIN

1 uncut loaf (1 pound) Italian peasant-style rustic bread or ciabatta bread

1/3 cup rosemary-flavored or plain olive oil

1/4 pound thinly sliced hard salami

1/4 pound thinly sliced prosciutto

1/4 pound sliced provolone cheese

1 small onion, thinly sliced

1. Cut bread loaf horizontally in half. Drizzle oil over cut sides of bread.

2. Layer salami, prosciutto, cheese and onion on bottom of bread; add top of bread. Cut loaf into 6 pieces. Serve immediately, or wrap securely with plastic wrap and refrigerate up to 24 hours to grab 'n go.

1 SANDWICH: Calories 735 (Calories from Fat 380); Fat 42g (Saturated 13g); Cholesterol 65mg; Sodium 1890mg; Carbohydrate 59g (Dietary Fiber 3g); Protein 30g • % Daily Value: Vitamin A 6%; Vitamin C 2%; Calcium 30%; Iron 24% • Exchanges: 4 Starch, 2 1/2 High-Fat Meat, 3 1/2 Fat • Carbohydrate Choices: 4

together time

Look at photos of the kids when they were younger, of you when you were small or of family members that you don't see very often. Kids will get a kick out of old fashions and hairdos and how people have changed.

Club Kaiser Sandwiches

6 SANDWICHES PREP: 20 MIN

1/4 cup sour cream

1 tablespoon chopped fresh basil leaves

2 tablespoons mayonnaise or salad dressing

1 tablespoon Worcestershire sauce

1 clove garlic, finely chopped

6 kaiser rolls, split

1/2 pound very thinly sliced baked ham

1/2 pound very thinly sliced oven-roasted turkey

1 1/2 cups fresh spinach leaves, stems removed

1 large tomato, cut into 6 slices

6 slices bacon, cooked and crumbled

1. Mix sour cream, basil, mayonnaise, Worcestershire sauce and garlic in small bowl. Cover and refrigerate 10 minutes to blend flavors.
2. Spread about 1 tablespoon sour cream mixture on cut sides of rolls. Layer bottom halves of rolls with ham, turkey, spinach, tomato and crumbled bacon. Cover with top halves of rolls. Serve immediately, or wrap securely with plastic wrap and refrigerate up to 24 hours to grab 'n go.

1 SANDWICH: Calories 335 (Calories from Fat 125); Fat 14g (Saturated 4g); Cholesterol 50mg; Sodium 1340mg; Carbohydrate 30g (Dietary Fiber 2g); Protein 22g • % Daily Value: Vitamin A 20%; Vitamin C 14%; Calcium 8%; Iron 16% • Exchanges: 2 Starch, 2 Lean Meat, 1 1/2 Fat • Carbohydrate Choices: 2

together time

Twist 'n shout. Have the kids twist the bacon slices a few times before you cook it. Bacon is a kid favorite, and the twisted shape adds a little more fun.

Club Kaiser Sandwiches

Family Heroes

4 SANDWICHES   PREP: 10 MIN

1/4 cup reduced-fat Thousand Island dressing

4 hoagie buns, split

4 large lettuce leaves

1/2 pound sliced cooked deli turkey

8 thin slices tomato (about 1 large)

2 ounces sliced hard salami

1 small cucumber, thinly sliced

2 slices (3/4 ounce each) process American cheese, cut in half

1. Spread dressing evenly on cut sides of buns.
2. Layer bottom halves of buns with lettuce, turkey, tomato, salami, cucumber and cheese. Cover with top halves of buns. Serve immediately, or wrap securely with plastic wrap and refrigerate up to 24 hours to grab 'n go.

1 SANDWICH: Calories 490 (Calories from Fat 155); Fat 17g (Saturated 6g); Cholesterol 70mg; Sodium 1180mg; Carbohydrate 52g (Dietary Fiber 3g); Protein 32g • % Daily Value: Vitamin A 6%; Vitamin C 4%; Calcium 16%; Iron 20% • Exchanges: 3 Starch, 1 Vegetable, 3 Medium-Fat Meat • Carbohydrate Choices: 3

together time

Roll Along. Do evening activities have you running? No problem! You'll be on a roll with these made-to-travel sandwiches. Remember to bring along a drink.

Turkey-Cucumber Sandwiches

4 SANDWICHES PREP: 15 MIN

1/4 cup mayonnaise or salad dressing

8 slices multigrain bread

1/2 pound sliced cooked deli turkey

4 slices (1 ounce each) dill Havarti or Muenster cheese

16 thin slices cucumber

4 lettuce leaves

1. Spread mayonnaise on one side of each bread slice.
2. Top 4 bread slices with turkey, cheese, cucumber and lettuce. Top with remaining bread. Serve immediately, or wrap securely with plastic wrap and refrigerate up to 24 hours to grab 'n go.

1 SANDWICH: Calories 420 (Calories from Fat 215); Fat 24g (Saturated 9g); Cholesterol 65mg; Sodium 1200mg; Carbohydrate 28g (Dietary Fiber 4g); Protein 23g • % Daily Value: Vitamin A 14%; Vitamin C 8%; Calcium 22%; Iron 16% • Exchanges: 2 Starch, 2 1/2 High-Fat Meat • Carbohydrate Choices: 2

together time

Search the sky for clouds. What shapes are they in? What animals, other creatures or pictures do you see in them? How fast do they blow away?

Turkey-Cheese Wraps

4 WRAPS PREP: 15 MIN

1 container (4 ounces) herb-and-garlic spreadable cheese

4 flour tortillas (8 to 10 inches in diameter)

8 ounces thinly sliced smoked turkey

4 ounces thinly sliced provolone cheese

1 cup shredded lettuce

1. Spread herb-and-garlic spreadable cheese over each tortilla. Top with turkey, cheese and lettuce to within 1 inch of edge.
2. Roll up tortillas tightly. Serve immediately, or wrap securely with plastic wrap and refrigerate up to 24 hours to grab 'n go.

1 WRAP: Calories 400 (Calories from Fat 200); Fat 22g (Saturated 12g); Cholesterol 75mg; Sodium 1210mg; Carbohydrate 27g (Dietary Fiber 2g); Protein 23g • % Daily Value: Vitamin A 8%; Vitamin C 0%; Calcium 8%; Iron 12% • Exchanges: 2 Starch, 1 1/2 Medium-Fat Meat, 3 Fat • Carbohydrate Choices: 2

together time

Have the kids color or decorate the outside of brown or white lunch bags while you make sandwiches. Pack dinner in the bag they've prepared, and take it along to eat on the way to soccer practice or piano lessons. Remember to bring along drinks.

Turkey-Cheese Wraps

Double-Wrapped Turkey Tacos

5 SERVINGS PREP: 10 MIN COOK: 15 MIN

1 pound ground turkey or ground beef

1 cup salsa

10 taco shells

1 container (6 ounces) frozen avocado dip, thawed, or 1 cup refried beans, heated

10 flour tortillas (6 inches in diameter)

1 cup shredded Cheddar cheese (4 ounces)

Shredded lettuce

1 large tomato, chopped (1 cup)

1. Cook turkey in 10-inch skillet over medium heat, about 5 minutes, stirring occasionally, until no longer pink; drain. Stir in salsa; reduce heat. Simmer uncovered 5 to 10 minutes to blend flavors.
2. Heat taco shells as directed on package. Spread about 1 tablespoon avocado dip over each tortilla to within 1 inch of edge. Place taco shell on avocado dip in center of tortilla. Wrap flour tortilla up sides of taco shell.
3. Sprinkle cheese into taco shells. Spoon turkey mixture into taco shells. Top with lettuce and tomato. Serve immediately, or wrap securely with plastic wrap and refrigerate up to 24 hours to grab 'n go.

2 TACOS: Calories 535 (Calories from Fat 225); Fat 25g (Saturated 8g); Cholesterol 85mg; Sodium 870mg; Carbohydrate 51g (Dietary Fiber 6g); Protein 33g • % Daily Value: Vitamin A 22%; Vitamin C 40%; Calcium 26%; Iron 24% • Exchanges: 3 Starch, 1 Vegetable, 3 Medium-Fat Meat, 3 Fat • Carbohydrate Choices: 3 1/2

together time

Keep the kids busy when you're driving by thinking of simple road games to play. Try the A to Z "I'm going on a trip and I'm taking a ________" memory game, limiting the items to foods packed for travel or camping.

Turkey-Jalapeño Quesadillas

4 QUESADILLAS   PREP: 10 MIN   COOK: 10 MIN

1/4 cup sour cream

1 tablespoon chopped fresh cilantro

1 envelope (1 1/4 ounces) taco seasoning mix

1/2 pound sliced cooked deli turkey

1 cup shredded Mexican cheese blend (4 ounces)

4 medium jalapeño chilies, seeded and coarsely chopped (1/4 cup)

4 flour tortillas (10 inches in diameter)

2 teaspoons vegetable oil

1. Mix sour cream, cilantro and taco seasoning mix in small container; cover with lid and set aside.
2. Layer turkey, cheese and chilies on 2 of the tortillas. Top with remaining tortillas. Brush top of each quesadilla with about 1/2 teaspoon of the oil.
3. Spray 10-inch nonstick skillet with cooking spray; heat over medium heat. Place 1 quesadilla, oil side down, in skillet; brush top with about 1/2 teaspoon oil. Cook about 2 minutes or until light golden brown. Turn quesadilla; cook 2 minutes longer or until light golden brown.
4. Repeat with remaining quesadilla. Cut into wedges. Serve immediately, or wrap securely with plastic wrap and refrigerate up to 24 hours to grab 'n go with sour cream mixture.

1 QUESADILLA: Calories 430 (Calories from Fat 170); Fat 19g (Saturated 8g); Cholesterol 60mg; Sodium 1270mg; Carbohydrate 41g (Dietary Fiber 3g); Protein 24g • % Daily Value: Vitamin A 12%; Vitamin C 6%; Calcium 28%; Iron 16% • Exchanges: 3 Starch, 2 Medium-Fat Meat, 1 Fat • Carbohydrate Choices: 3

together time

Make faces. Let the kids create faces with foods such as sliced olives for eyes, a baby carrot for a nose, half of a bell pepper for a mouth and shredded cheese for hair. It's fun, colorful and adds veggies to the meal.

family fun

ASIAN NIGHT

You can stir up an interest in ethnic foods by making family meals a fun and exciting experience. Visit an Asian market together to look for new ingredients. Why not purchase a fresh or canned fruit that's new to your family, such as litchis or Asian pears, for dessert?

Menu

Egg Rolls (at right)

Cantonese Chicken Chop Suey (page 31)

Sesame Pea Pods (at right)

Kiwifruit with Orange and Chocolate (at right)

Corbis Digital Stock

Egg Rolls

Heat purchased **frozen egg rolls** as directed on package. Serve with **sweet-and-sour sauce** and **hot mustard**.

Sesame Pea Pods

Heat 1 tablespoon **sesame oil** in 10-inch skillet over medium-high heat. Add 1/2 pound **snow (Chinese) pea pods** (2 cups) and 1 tablespoon **sesame seed**. Cook about 2 minutes, stirring frequently, until pea pods are crisp-tender. Stir in 1 medium **red or yellow bell pepper**, cut into thin strips. Cook about 2 minutes, stirring frequently, until bell pepper is crisp-tender.

Kiwifruit with Orange and Chocolate

Mix 1 cup **orange or plain yogurt** with 2 tablespoons frozen (partially thawed) **orange juice concentrate**. Spoon 1/4 cup yogurt mixture onto each of 4 dessert plates. Peel 4 large **kiwifruit**; cut into 1/4-inch slices. Arrange kiwifruit on yogurt mixture. Melt 1/4 cup **semisweet chocolate chips** and 2 teaspoons **shortening** over low heat, stirring constantly. Carefully drizzle chocolate in thin lines over kiwifruit.

More Asian Ideas

Want to check out something different than chop suey? Try these other Asian dishes instead.

Orange Teriyaki Beef with Noodles (page 13)

Asian Chicken Roll-Ups (page 90)

Honey Barbecue Pork Roast with Carrots and Corn (page 121)

Crab and Spinach Casserole (page 185)

helping is fun

Mom or Dad

- Makes chop suey
- Stir-fries sesame pea pods
- Peels and slices kiwifruit

The Kids:

- Set out sauces for egg rolls
- Measure cashews for chop suey
- Mix yogurt and o.j. concentrate for dessert

together time

Finish with a fruit fondue. Make or buy sweet drizzling or dipping sauces and let everyone decorate their own fresh or canned fruits, like kiwis, tangerines or mandarin slices, mangos, pineapple, Asian pears and litchis.

Have fun reading your fortunes. You can buy fortune cookies in an Asian market and some supermarkets. Or buy thin, rolled cookies, write fortunes on small slips of paper and insert them inside.

Turn the kids into chopstick pros with this easy invention! Wrap a rubber band around two chopsticks, near the tops. Fold a business card into a small square, and place it between the chopsticks with the fold just below the rubber band. The rubber band and card work like a spring to make using the chopsticks easy!

Asian Chicken Roll-Ups

4 ROLL-UPS PREP: 15 MIN

- 2 tablespoons crunchy peanut butter
- 2 tablespoons teriyaki baste and glaze (from 12-ounce bottle)
- 1 tablespoon packed brown sugar
- 1 tablespoon hot water
- 1 teaspoon sesame oil or vegetable oil
- 4 flour tortillas (8 to 10 inches in diameter)
- 8 slices sliced cooked deli chicken breast
- 1 1/2 cups shredded iceberg lettuce or broccoli slaw
- 1 1/2 cups shredded carrots
- 1/2 cup chopped fresh cilantro

1. Beat peanut butter, teriyaki baste and glaze, brown sugar, water and oil in small bowl with wire whisk until smooth.

2. Spread about 2 tablespoons peanut butter mixture over each tortilla. Top each with 2 slices chicken, about 1/3 cup lettuce, about 1/3 cup carrots and 2 tablespoons cilantro. Roll up tightly. Serve immediately, or wrap securely with plastic wrap and refrigerate up to 24 hours to grab 'n go.

1 ROLL-UP: Calories 280 (Calories from Fat 90); Fat 10g (Saturated 2g); Cholesterol 25mg; Sodium 630mg; Carbohydrate 35g (Dietary Fiber 4g); Protein 16g • % Daily Value: Vitamin A 100%; Vitamin C 10%; Calcium 8%; Iron 14% • Exchanges: 2 Starch, 1 Lean Meat, 1 Vegetable, 1 Fat • Carbohydrate Choices: 2

together time

Fill an empty shoe box with several small objects from around the house. Without looking, have each family member pick an object from the box and tell a story about it.

Asian Chicken Roll-Ups

Chicken Salad in Pitas

4 PITA HALVES   PREP: 15 MIN

2 pita breads (6 inches in diameter)

2 cups chopped cooked chicken breast

1 cup frozen green peas, thawed and drained

1/2 cup mayonnaise or salad dressing

1/4 teaspoon salt

1/4 teaspoon pepper

1 medium stalk celery, chopped (1/2 cup)

4 medium green onions, sliced (1/4 cup)

1 small mango, peeled, pitted and diced (3/4 cup)

1. Cut pita breads in half; open to form pockets. Mix remaining ingredients in large bowl.
2. Divide chicken mixture among pita bread halves. Serve immediately, or wrap securely with plastic wrap and refrigerate up to 24 hours to grab 'n go.

1/2 PITA: Calories 440 (Calories from Fat 225); Fat 25g (Saturated 4g); Cholesterol 75mg; Sodium 520mg; Carbohydrate 28g (Dietary Fiber 4g); Protein 25g • % Daily Value: Vitamin A 14%; Vitamin C 34%; Calcium 6%; Iron 12% • Exchanges: 2 Starch, 2 High-Fat Meat, 2 Fat • Carbohydrate Choices: 2

together time

Transport this meal to the video room for a relaxing night huddled together watching family-favorite videos. Set aside Fridays to view a series of comedies or mysteries.

Shrimp and Egg Salad Wraps

4 WRAPS PREP: 10 MIN

- 4 hard-cooked eggs, peeled and chopped
- 1 cup chopped cooked shrimp
- 2 tablespoons finely chopped red onion
- 3 tablespoons creamy mustard-mayonnaise sauce
- 1/4 teaspoon salt
- 4 flour tortillas (8 inches in diameter)
- 2 cups shredded lettuce

1. Mix all ingredients except tortillas and lettuce in medium bowl.
2. Spread shrimp mixture evenly on each tortilla; top with lettuce. Fold in sides of each wrap; roll up. Cut each in half. Serve immediately, or wrap securely with plastic wrap and refrigerate up to 24 hours to grab 'n go.

1 WRAP: **Calories 330 (Calories from Fat 135); Fat 15g (Saturated 3g); Cholesterol 335mg; Sodium 640mg; Carbohydrate 21g (Dietary Fiber 2g); Protein 23g • % Daily Value: Vitamin A 10%; Vitamin C 4%; Calcium 10%; Iron 22% • Exchanges: 2 Starch, 2 Lean Meat, 1 1/2 Fat • Carbohydrate Choices: 1 1/2**

together time

Play your favorite classical music during dinner. Listening to classical music stimulates and helps develop a creative part of children's brains. It also introduces them to a wide range of music.

Caesar Salad Wraps

4 WRAPS PREP: 15 MIN

16 small romaine lettuce leaves

1/4 cup chopped red onion

2 tablespoons shredded Parmesan or Romano cheese

1/4 cup Caesar dressing

4 garden vegetable–flavored flour tortillas (6 or 8 inches in diameter)

4 hard-cooked eggs, sliced

2 roma (plum) tomatoes, sliced

1. Toss romaine, onion, cheese and dressing. Place romaine mixture evenly down center of each tortilla. Top with eggs and tomatoes.
2. Fold up one end of tortilla about 1 inch over filling; fold right and left sides over folded end, overlapping. Fold remaining end down; secure with toothpick if necessary. Serve immediately, or wrap securely with plastic wrap and refrigerate up to 24 hours to grab 'n go.

1 WRAP: Calories 240 (Calories from Fat 125); Fat 14g (Saturated 3g); Cholesterol 215mg; Sodium 390mg; Carbohydrate 19g (Dietary Fiber 2g); Protein 11g • % Daily Value: Vitamin A 32%; Vitamin C 30%; Calcium 12%; Iron 12% • Exchanges: 1 Starch, 1 High-Fat Meat, 1 Vegetable, 1 Fat • Carbohydrate Choices: 1

together time

Wrap up these kid-favorite sandwiches, pack the wagon or bicycles with juice boxes and individual containers of applesauce, and roll on down to the park or beach for a fun afternoon. A blanket is handy for spreading the picnic as well as for nap time!

Veggies and Cheese Mini Pizzas

4 MINI PIZZAS   PREP: 5 MIN   BAKE: 12 MIN

4 pita breads (6 inches in diameter)

4 roma (plum) tomatoes, chopped (1 cup)

2 small zucchini, chopped (2 cups)

1 small onion, chopped (1/4 cup)

1/4 cup sliced ripe olives

2 teaspoons chopped fresh or 1/2 teaspoon dried basil leaves

1/2 cup spaghetti sauce or pizza sauce

1 cup shredded mozzarella cheese (4 ounces)

1. Heat oven to 425°. Split pita breads in half around edge with knife. Place rounds on ungreased cookie sheet. Bake about 5 minutes or just until crisp.
2. Mix tomatoes, zucchini, onion, olives and basil in medium bowl. Spread spaghetti sauce evenly over pita rounds. Top with vegetable mixture. Sprinkle with cheese.
3. Bake 5 to 7 minutes or until cheese is melted. Cut into wedges. Serve immediately, or wrap securely with plastic wrap and refrigerate up to 24 hours to grab 'n go.

1 MINI PIZZA: Calories 290 (Calories from Fat 70); Fat 8g (Saturated 3g); Cholesterol 15mg; Sodium 660mg; Carbohydrate 41g (Dietary Fiber 3g); Protein 14g • % Daily Value: Vitamin A 26%; Vitamin C 36%; Calcium 28%; Iron 14% • Exchanges: 2 Starch, 2 Vegetable, 1/2 Medium-Fat Meat, 1 Fat • Carbohydrate Choices: 3

together time

Figure it out! How many times do you need to cut the pizza to get 8 wedges? Kids can easily solve this math question—plus, they'll be able to handle smaller pieces more easily.

Chapter 4

Steady Cooking with the Slow Cooker

It takes just a few minutes in the morning, then your slow cooker simmers during the day while you're at work and the kids are at school. (If your work is at home, the slow cooker stays busy cooking your dinner.) You'll come home to cozy food aromas wafting through the house, and in precious little time, with no panic, dinner's ready and waiting for you.

Savory Chicken and Vegetables (page 98)

Savory Chicken and Vegetables

Photo on page 97

8 SERVINGS PREP: 20 MIN COOK: 10 HR 30 MIN

8 boneless, skinless chicken thighs (about 1 1/2 pounds)

2 cups chicken broth

1 teaspoon salt

1/4 teaspoon pepper

8 ounces pearl onions

6 slices bacon, cooked and crumbled

2 cloves garlic, finely chopped

Bouquet Garni (see note)

1 bag (1 pound) baby-cut carrots

1 pound small whole button mushrooms

2 tablespoons all-purpose flour

2 tablespoons cold water

1. Place chicken in 5- to 6-quart slow cooker. Add remaining ingredients except mushrooms, flour and water.
2. Cover and cook on low heat setting 8 to 10 hours.
3. Skim any fat from surface. Remove Bouquet Garni. Stir in mushrooms. Mix flour and cold water; stir into chicken mixture. Increase heat setting to high. Cover and cook about 30 minutes or until thickened.

Note: To make Bouquet Garni: Tie 4 sprigs parsley, 2 dried bay leaves and 1 teaspoon dried thyme leaves in cheesecloth bag or place in tea ball.

1 SERVING: Calories 200 (Calories from Fat 70); Fat 8g (Saturated 3g); Cholesterol 45mg; Sodium 690mg; Carbohydrate 12g (Dietary Fiber 3g); Protein 20g • % Daily Value: Vitamin A 100%; Vitamin C 6%; Calcium 4%; Iron 12% • Exchanges: 2 Lean Meat, 2 Vegetable, 1/2 Fat • Carbohydrate Choices: 1

together time

Set up a fondue for dessert! Get out the chocolate chips and melt them in the fondue pot or microwave. Let everyone have their own custard cup of melted chocolate with lots of dunkers such as fresh fruit, pieces of cupcakes or cut-up angel food cake.

Chicken and Vegetables with Dumplings

8 SERVINGS PREP: 10 MIN COOK: 10 HR 50 MIN

2 1/2 to 3 pounds boneless skinless chicken thighs

1 pound small red potatoes (about 2 1/2 inches in diameter)

1 medium onion, coarsely chopped (3/4 cup)

2 cups baby-cut carrots

3 cans (14 ounces each) chicken broth

2 cups Original Bisquick mix

1/2 cup water

2 teaspoons parsley flakes

1. Place chicken, potatoes, onion and carrots in 6-quart slow cooker. Add broth.
2. Cover and cook on low heat setting 9 to 10 hours.
3. Increase heat setting to high. Stir together Bisquick mix, water and parsley in medium bowl. Drop dough by rounded tablespoonfuls onto hot chicken mixture. Cover and cook 45 to 50 minutes or until dumplings are dry in center.

1 SERVING: **Calories 425 (Calories from Fat 145); Fat 16g (Saturated 5g); Cholesterol 90mg; Sodium 970mg; Carbohydrate 35g (Dietary Fiber 3g); Protein 35g • % Daily Value: Vitamin A 100%; Vitamin C 8%; Calcium 10%; Iron 24% • Exchanges: 2 Starch, 1 Vegetable, 4 Lean Meat, 1/2 Fat • Carbohydrate Choices: 4**

together time

Spread a blanket on the lawn after dark, lie on your back and gaze up into the night sky. Can you spot the Big Dipper? How about the Little Dipper? Any other constellations? Now try it with binoculars to see how many you can find!

Grandma's Chicken Noodle Soup

6 SERVINGS PREP: 30 MIN COOK: 7 HR 10 MIN

3/4 pound boneless, skinless chicken thighs, cut into 1-inch pieces

2 medium stalks celery (with leaves), sliced (1 1/4 cups)

1 large carrot, chopped (3/4 cup)

1 medium onion, chopped (1/2 cup)

1 can (14 1/2 ounces) diced tomatoes, undrained

1 can (14 ounces) chicken broth

1 teaspoon dried thyme leaves

1 package (10 ounces) frozen green peas

1 cup frozen home-style egg noodles (from 12-ounce bag) or 1 cup uncooked fine egg noodles or 1 cup uncooked instant rice

1 tablespoon chopped fresh parsley

1. Spray 10-inch skillet with cooking spray; heat over medium heat. Cook chicken in skillet about 5 minutes, stirring frequently, until brown.
2. Mix chicken and remaining ingredients except peas, noodles and parsley in 3 1/2- to 4-quart slow cooker.
3. Cover and cook on low heat setting 6 hours 30 minutes to 7 hours.
4. Stir in peas and noodles. Cover and cook on low heat setting about 10 minutes or until noodles are tender. Stir in parsley just before serving.

1 SERVING: Calories 200 (Calories from Fat 55); Fat 6g (Saturated 2g); Cholesterol 45mg; Sodium 510mg; Carbohydrate 20g (Dietary Fiber 4g); Protein 20g • % Daily Value: Vitamin A 54%; Vitamin C 14%; Calcium 6%; Iron 16% • Exchanges: 1 Starch, 2 Very Lean Meat, 1 Vegetable, 1/2 Fat • Carbohydrate Choices: 1

together time

Find out which foods float and which foods sink when you set out toppers to add to soup. Try small crackers, popped popcorn, shelled sunflower nuts, bacon pieces, olives or bite-size pieces of cooked veggies. A yummy experiment!

Grandma's Chicken Noodle Soup

Mexican Chicken Tostadas

10 TOSTADAS PREP: 20 MIN COOK: 10 HR

1 large jalapeño chili, finely chopped

10 cloves garlic, finely chopped

2 tablespoons Mexican chili powder

2 tablespoons olive or vegetable oil

2 tablespoons lime juice

2 teaspoons salt

2 packages (1 1/4 pounds each) boneless, skinless chicken thighs

1 package (4.8 ounces) tostada shells (10 shells)

1 cup shredded lettuce

1 cup shredded Cheddar cheese (4 ounces)

3/4 cup salsa

1/4 cup sour cream

1. Mix jalapeño chili, garlic, chili powder, oil, lime juice and salt in 3- to 4-quart slow cooker. Add chicken; coat with oil mixture.
2. Cover and cook on low heat setting 8 to 10 hours.
3. Remove chicken from cooker; place on cutting board. Shred chicken, using two forks. Return chicken to cooker and mix well. Using slotted spoon to remove chicken mixture from cooker, place 1/3 cup chicken mixture on each tostada shell. Top with lettuce, cheese, salsa and sour cream.

1 TOSTADA: Calories 305 (Calories from Fat 155); Fat 17g (Saturated 6g); Cholesterol 85mg; Sodium 730mg; Carbohydrate 10g (Dietary Fiber 2g); Protein 28g • % Daily Value: Vitamin A 18%; Vitamin C 12%; Calcium 12%; Iron 14% • Exchanges: 1/2 Starch, 4 Lean Meat, 1 Fat • Carbohydrate Choices: 1/2

together time

Plant a vegetable garden! When deciding which vegetables you want to grow, let the kids pick out veggies that they like to eat. Kids can have fun picking out seeds, planting, weeding and harvesting their crops.

Upside-Down Chicken Pot Pie

8 SERVINGS PREP: 10 MIN COOK: 10 HR 15 MIN

1 1/4 pounds boneless, skinless chicken thighs

1 tablespoon instant chopped onion

1 dried bay leaf

1/4 teaspoon pepper

1 jar (18 ounces) chicken gravy

2 medium stalks celery, cut into 1/2-inch slices

2 1/4 cups Original Bisquick mix

2/3 cup milk

1 bag (1 pound) frozen mixed vegetables

1. Place chicken in 3 1/2- to 4-quart slow cooker. Top with onion, bay leaf, pepper and gravy. Place celery on gravy.
2. Cover and cook on low heat setting 8 to 10 hours.
3. About 30 minutes before serving, make and bake 8 biscuits using Bisquick mix and milk as directed on package.
4. Meanwhile, gently stir frozen vegetables into chicken mixture. Increase heat setting to high. Cover and cook 15 minutes. Remove bay leaf. For each serving, split biscuit and place in soup bowl or tart pan. Spoon about 3/4 cup chicken mixture on top of biscuit.

1 SERVING: Calories 335 (Calories from Fat 135); Fat 15g (Saturated 4g); Cholesterol 45mg; Sodium 940mg; Carbohydrate 29g (Dietary Fiber 3g); Protein 21g • % Daily Value: Vitamin A 42%; Vitamin C 16%; Calcium 14%; Iron 16% • Exchanges: 2 Starch, 2 Lean Meat, 1 1/2 Fat • Carbohydrate Choices: 2

together time

Help kids develop their sensory skills at dinner. Instead of answering them when they ask, "What's for dinner?" have them close their eyes and guess what it is by smelling, hearing (sizzling, simmering, etc.) or touching the foods before they are served.

family fun

RANCH NIGHT

Round up the family and turn dinnertime into a western-themed night. Let everyone wear bandanas and cowboy hats. Role-playing is a great way to encourage creative thinking and show kids it's fine (and fun) to be silly sometimes. Giddyup!

Menu

Beef and Bean Dinner *(page 162)*

Texas Toast (at right)

Ranch Vegetables (at right)

Trail Mix on Sticks (at right)

PhotoDisc/Getty Images

Texas Toast

Spread 1/4 cup **butter**, softened, on both sides of 3 slices **thick-cut white bread**. Sprinkle both sides with **seasoned salt**. Place on rack in broiler pan. Broil with tops 4 to 6 inches from heat 2 to 4 minutes, turning once, until lightly toasted. Sprinkle with 3/4 cup **shredded mozzarella cheese**; let stand 1 to 2 minutes to melt. Cut each slice diagonally in half.

Ranch Vegetables

Heat 1 tablespoon **olive or vegetable oil** in 10-inch nonstick skillet over medium-high heat. Add 1-pound bag **frozen vegetable combination** and 1/2 envelope (1 ounce) **ranch dressing mix** (milk recipe). Cover and cook 5 to 7 minutes, stirring frequently, until vegetables are crisp-tender.

Trail Mix on Sticks

Heat 3 cups **miniature marshmallows** and 1/4 cup **butter** in 3-quart saucepan over low heat, stirring constantly, until smooth. Stir in 1/4 cup **creamy peanut butter**. Remove from heat. Stir in 3 cups **Cheerios® cereal** and 1/3 cup **sunflower nuts** until coated. Let stand 2 minutes. Shape into 2-inch balls. Insert wooden stick into middle of each ball. Place on waxed paper. Let stand about 20 minutes or until firm.

More Ranch Ideas

Try these other ranch-style dishes.

Country Eggs in Tortilla Cups (page 55)
Southwestern Pot Roast (page 118)
Cowboy Chicken and Beans (page 132)
Ranch Chicken Patties (page 129)

helping is fun

Mom or Dad

- Prepares beef and bean dinner
- Heats oil for vegetables
- Heats marshmallow mixture

The Kids

- Spread butter and sprinkle cheese on toast
- Stir in vegetables and ranch dressing mix
- Mix cereal and nuts with marshmallow; shape into balls

together time

Tackle trail mix together and customize it to everyone's taste. Start with the suggested ingredients and add other favorites like raisins or dried cranberries, chopped walnuts or peanuts, chocolate chips, and shredded or flaked coconut.

Discuss the differences between a ranch and a farm. How many of the foods in the dinner you're eating come from a ranch and which are grown on a farm? What animals can you find on a ranch and which ones on a farm?

Pitch camp in your kitchen or dining room. Spread a blanket to sit on, and serve dinner on paper or plastic plates. Play nature tapes, if you have them.

Sing campfire songs together like "The Farmer in the Dell," "Home on the Range," "This Land is Your Land" and any other cowboy songs you know.

Italian Ground Turkey Sandwiches

12 SANDWICHES   PREP: 15 MIN   COOK: 5 HR

2 1/2 pounds lean ground turkey or beef

1 medium onion, chopped (1/2 cup)

2 teaspoons finely chopped garlic

1 jar (48 ounces) chunky garden vegetable pasta sauce

1 can (6 ounces) tomato paste

1 can (3.8 ounces) sliced ripe olives, drained

12 French rolls (6 inches), split

6 slices (1 ounce each) mozzarella cheese, cut in half

1. Spray 12-inch nonstick skillet with cooking spray; heat over medium-high heat. Cook turkey, onion and garlic in skillet about 8 minutes, stirring frequently, until turkey is no longer pink; drain.
2. Mix turkey mixture, pasta sauce, tomato paste and olives in 3 1/2- to 4-quart slow cooker.
3. Cover and cook on low heat setting 4 to 5 hours.
4. Fill each roll with 1/2 cup turkey mixture and half slice of cheese, cutting to fit.

1 SANDWICH: Calories 440 (Calories from Fat 130); Fat 15g (Saturated 4g); Cholesterol 70mg; Sodium 450mg; Carbohydrate 50g (Dietary Fiber 4g); Protein 31g • % Daily Value: Vitamin A 22%; Vitamin C 18%; Calcium 18%; Iron 20% • Exchanges: 2 Starch, 3 1/2 Medium-Fat Meat, 1 Vegetable • Carbohydrate Choices: 3

together time

Help new readers learn words by letting them cook dinner with you. Read out loud words on labels and recipes to help with new pronunciations. It's a whole new world when you can read!

Pizza Chicken

8 SERVINGS PREP: 10 MIN COOK: 6 HR

- 8 boneless, skinless chicken thighs (about 1 1/2 pounds) or 6 boneless pork chops, trimmed of fat
- 1/2 teaspoon salt
- 1/4 teaspoon pepper
- 1 small onion, sliced
- 2 medium yellow, red or green bell peppers, cut into strips
- 2 cups spaghetti sauce
- 1 package (16 ounces) rotini pasta
- 1 cup shredded mozzarella cheese (4 ounces)

1. Sprinkle chicken with salt and pepper. (If using pork chops, brown the pork chops in 12-inch skillet over medium heat, then continue as directed.) Place chicken in 3 1/2- to 6-quart slow cooker. Top with onion and bell peppers. Add spaghetti sauce.
2. Cover and cook on low heat setting 4 to 6 hours.
3. Cook and drain pasta as directed on package. Place pasta on platter. Top with chicken and sauce. Sprinkle with cheese.

1 SERVING: Calories 405 (Calories from Fat 100); Fat 11g (Saturated 4g); Cholesterol 50mg; Sodium 570mg; Carbohydrate 54g (Dietary Fiber 3g); Protein 26g • % Daily Value: Vitamin A 12%; Vitamin C 30%; Calcium 14%; Iron 22% • Exchanges: 3 Starch, 2 Vegetable, 2 Medium-Fat Meat • Carbohydrate Choices: 3 1/2

together time

Learn to appreciate music by accompanying dinner with some new tunes. Investigate a style of music you'd like to know better. Borrow CDs from the library, or dust off some forgotten selections from your own collection.

Sloppy Joes

24 BUNS PREP: 20 MIN COOK: 9 HR 10 MIN
(or enough Sloppy Joes for 3 recipes, about 2 1/2 cups each)

3 pounds ground turkey or beef

1 large onion, coarsely chopped (1 cup)

1 1/2 medium stalks celery, chopped (1 1/2 cups)

1 cup barbecue sauce

1 can (26 1/2 ounces) sloppy joe sauce

24 hamburger buns

1. Cook turkey and onion in 4-quart Dutch oven over medium heat about 10 minutes, stirring occasionally, until turkey is no longer pink; drain.
2. Mix turkey mixture and remaining ingredients except buns in 3 1/2- to 6-quart slow cooker.
3. Cover and cook on low heat setting 7 to 9 hours.
4. Increase heat setting to high. Uncover and cook 5 to 10 minutes or until desired consistency. Stir well before serving. Fill buns with turkey mixture.

1 BUN: Calories 255 (Calories from Fat 45); Fat 5g (Saturated 1g); Cholesterol 35mg; Sodium 750mg; Carbohydrate 35g (Dietary Fiber 2g); Protein 17g • % Daily Value: Vitamin A 8%; Vitamin C 4%; Calcium 8%; Iron 12% • Exchanges: 2 Starch, 1 Vegetable, 1 Medium-Fat Meat • Carbohydrate Choices: 2

together time

Let the kids top their own Sloppy Joes with a slice of cheese before adding the top of the bun. Not only does it taste great, but as the cheese melts, it helps hold the mixture together so it can't escape. The result? Tidy Joes!

Sloppy Joes

Taco Shortcakes

12 SHORTCAKES PREP: 25 MIN COOK: 10 HR

2-pound pork boneless shoulder roast, trimmed of fat

1 envelope (1 1/4 ounces) taco seasoning mix

1 can (16 ounces) refried beans

8 ounces mild Mexican-style process cheese spread loaf, cubed

12 prepared corn muffins

3/4 cup shredded lettuce

3/4 cup chopped tomato

3/4 cup sour cream

1/4 cup chopped fresh cilantro

1. If pork is tied, remove strings or netting. Place pork in 3- to 4-quart slow cooker. Sprinkle with taco seasoning mix. Top with beans.
2. Cover and cook on low heat setting 8 to 10 hours.
3. Remove pork from cooker; place on cutting board. Shred pork, using 2 forks. Return pork to cooker and mix well. Stir in cheese.
4. To serve, cut muffins crosswise in half. Place each bottom half on plate; top with 1/2 cup pork mixture, 1 tablespoon lettuce, 1 tablespoon tomato and muffin top. Top each shortcake with 1 tablespoon sour cream; sprinkle with cilantro.

1 SHORTCAKE: Calories 470 (Calories from Fat 200); Fat 22g (Saturated 10g); Cholesterol 110mg; Sodium 930mg; Carbohydrate 41g (Dietary Fiber 4g); Protein 26g • % Daily Value: Vitamin A 14%; Vitamin C 4%; Calcium 22%; Iron 14% • Exchanges: 2 1/2 Starch, 1 Vegetable, 3 Medium-Fat Meat, 1/2 Fat • Carbohydrate Choices: 3

together time

Serve Cinnamon "Fried" Ice Cream, page 49, for a fiesta finale to a Mexican meal. Kids can help make the dessert while you sneak in a geography lesson.

Open-Face Turkey Diner Sandwiches

6 SANDWICHES   PREP: 15 MIN   COOK: 10 HR

1 package (2 pounds) turkey breast tenderloins

1/2 teaspoon rubbed sage

2 jars (12 ounces each) roasted turkey gravy

1 package (28 ounces) frozen home-style mashed potatoes or instant mashed potato mix

1/2 teaspoon poultry seasoning

1 teaspoon Worcestershire sauce

6 slices white bread, toasted

Paprika

1. Place turkey in 3- to 4-quart slow cooker. Sprinkle with sage. Top with gravy.
2. Cover and cook on low heat setting 8 to 10 hours.
3. About 10 minutes before serving, cook mashed potatoes as directed on package for 3 servings.
4. Remove turkey from cooker; place on cutting board. Cut turkey into 12 pieces. Stir poultry seasoning and Worcestershire sauce into gravy in cooker. Place 2 pieces turkey on each toast slice. Top with 1/4 cup mashed potatoes. Spoon gravy over potatoes. Sprinkle with paprika.

1 SANDWICH: Calories 480 (Calories from Fat 145); Fat 16g (Saturated 4g); Cholesterol 105mg; Sodium 1160mg; Carbohydrate 41g (Dietary Fiber 3g); Protein 42g • % Daily Value: Vitamin A 24%; Vitamin C 6%; Calcium 10%; Iron 20% • Exchanges: 3 Starch, 4 1/2 Lean Meat • Carbohydrate Choices: 3

together time

Make an erupting kitchen volcano. Let the kids mix white vinegar and baking soda, then watch the chemical reaction as carbon dioxide bubbles up. (If you do it over the sink your drain will get clean, too!)

Barbecue Beef Sandwiches

12 SANDWICHES PREP: 20 MIN COOK: 8 HR 30 MIN

3-pound beef boneless chuck roast, trimmed of fat

1 cup barbecue sauce

1/2 cup apricot, orange or peach preserves

2 tablespoons chopped red or green bell pepper

1 tablespoon Dijon mustard

2 teaspoons packed brown sugar

1 small onion, sliced

12 kaiser or hamburger buns, split

1. Cut beef into 4 pieces. Place beef in 4- to 5-quart slow cooker. Mix remaining ingredients except buns; pour over beef.
2. Cover and cook on low heat setting 7 to 8 hours.
3. Remove beef from cooker; place on cutting board. Cut beef into thin slices. Stir beef into sauce in cooker. Cover and cook on low heat setting 20 to 30 minutes or until beef is hot. Fill buns with beef mixture.

1 SANDWICH: Calories 425 (Calories from Fat 135); Fat 15g (Saturated 5g); Cholesterol 70mg; Sodium 570mg; Carbohydrate 44g (Dietary Fiber 2g); Protein 28g • % Daily Value: Vitamin A 4%; Vitamin C 4%; Calcium 6%; Iron 24% • Exchanges: 2 Starch, 1 Other Carbohydrate, 3 Lean Meat, 1 Fat • Carbohydrate Choices: 3

together time

Make marbled milk by pouring a little chocolate or strawberry syrup on top of milk in glasses. As it sinks into the milk, the milk will look marbled. Awesome refreshment!

Barbecue Beef Sandwiches

Italian Beef Stew

6 SERVINGS PREP: 15 MIN COOK: 12 HR 15 MIN

- 1 pound beef stew meat
- 3 large carrots, cut into 1-inch pieces (2 cups)
- 2 medium stalks celery, cut into 1-inch pieces (1 1/2 cups)
- 2 cloves garlic, finely chopped
- 1 medium onion, coarsely chopped (1 1/2 cups)
- 1 can (19 ounces) cannellini (white kidney) beans or 1 can (15 to 16 ounces) red kidney beans, rinsed and drained
- 1 can (28 ounces) crushed tomatoes in puree, undrained
- 1 jar (12 ounces) beef gravy
- 2 teaspoons Italian seasoning
- 1 teaspoon sugar
- 2 cups frozen cut green beans (from 1-pound bag)

1. Place beef, carrots, celery, garlic, onion, beans, tomatoes and gravy in order listed in 3 1/2- to 4-quart slow cooker.
2. Cover and cook on low heat setting 10 to 12 hours.
3. Stir in Italian seasoning, sugar and frozen green beans. Increase heat setting to high. Cover and cook about 15 minutes or until green beans are tender.

1 SERVING: Calories 325 (Calories from Fat 100); Fat 11g (Saturated 4g); Cholesterol 50mg; Sodium 800mg; Carbohydrate 38g (Dietary Fiber 10g); Protein 28g • % Daily Value: Vitamin A 100%; Vitamin C 22%; Calcium 12%; Iron 34% • Exchanges: 2 Starch, 2 Vegetable, 2 1/2 Very Lean Meat • Carbohydrate Choices: 2 1/2

together time

Reinforce the importance of family dinner-time by letting the phone ring or letting the answering machine pick up phone calls while you're eating.

Saucy Short Ribs

6 SERVINGS PREP: 10 MIN COOK: 9 HR

3 1/2 to 4 pounds beef short ribs, cut into pieces

1/2 teaspoon seasoned salt

1/4 teaspoon pepper

1 medium onion, cut into thin wedges

1 can (10 3/4 ounces) condensed cream of celery soup

1/2 cup chili sauce

1 tablespoon Worcestershire sauce

1. Sprinkle ribs with seasoned salt and pepper. Layer ribs and onion in 3 1/2- to 4-quart slow cooker. Mix remaining ingredients in small bowl; pour over ribs.
2. Cover and cook on low heat setting 7 to 9 hours. Serve sauce over ribs.

1 SERVING: Calories 295 (Calories from Fat 160); Fat 18g (Saturated 7g); Cholesterol 60mg; Sodium 830mg; Carbohydrate 12g (Dietary Fiber 1g); Protein 21g • % Daily Value: Vitamin A 10%; Vitamin C 4%; Calcium 4%; Iron 12% • Exchanges: 1 Starch, 2 1/2 Medium-Fat Meat, 1/2 Fat • Carbohydrate Choices: 1

together time

Make ice-cream shakes! Whip them up quickly in your blender with vanilla ice cream, a squirt of chocolate syrup and enough milk to make them drinkable through a straw. Yum!

Fajita Beef Dinner

8 SERVINGS PREP: 10 MIN COOK: 9 HR 15 MIN

2 1/2-pound beef boneless top round steak, trimmed of fat

1 large onion, cut in half and sliced

1 can (14 1/2 ounces) stewed tomatoes, undrained

1 envelope (1.12 ounces) fajita seasoning mix

1 medium red bell pepper, cut into 1-inch pieces

1 medium green bell pepper, cut into 1-inch pieces

4 cups uncooked instant rice

4 1/4 cups water

1/4 cup all-purpose flour

1. Cut beef into 2-inch pieces. Mix beef and onion in 3 1/2- to 4-quart slow cooker. Mix tomatoes and fajita seasoning mix in small bowl; pour over beef mixture. Top with bell peppers.
2. Cover and cook on low heat setting 7 to 9 hours.
3. Cook rice in 4 cups of the water as directed on package. Meanwhile, mix remaining 1/4 cup water and the flour; gradually stir into beef mixture in cooker. Increase heat setting to high. Cover and cook about 15 minutes, stirring occasionally, until thickened. Serve over rice.

1 SERVING: Calories 380 (Calories from Fat 45); Fat 5g (Saturated 2g); Cholesterol 75mg; Sodium 220mg; Carbohydrate 56g (Dietary Fiber 4g); Protein 34g • % Daily Value: Vitamin A 10%; Vitamin C 24%; Calcium 4%; Iron 28% • Exchanges: 3 Starch, 3 Very Lean Meat, 2 Vegetable • Carbohydrate Choices: 4

together time

Pretend you're in Mexico and you're part of a fiesta! Let the kids make colorful decorations, play fiesta music or form a kitchen band. Olé!

Hearty Beef Chili

10 SERVINGS PREP: 10 MIN COOK: 9 HR

2 pounds beef stew meat

1 envelope (1 ounce) onion soup mix (from 2-ounce package)

5 teaspoons chili powder

1 teaspoon ground cumin

1 can (15 1/2 ounces) kidney beans, rinsed and drained

2 cans (10 ounces each) diced tomatoes and mild green chiles, undrained

1 can (15 ounces) tomato sauce

1 can (14 1/2 ounces) diced tomatoes, undrained

1. Place all ingredients in order listed in 3 1/2- to 4-quart slow cooker.
2. Cover and cook on low heat setting 8 to 9 hours.
3. Stir gently to mix before serving.

1 SERVING: Calories 255 (Calories from Fat 100); Fat 11g (Saturated 4g); Cholesterol 55mg; Sodium 840mg; Carbohydrate 20g (Dietary Fiber 5g); Protein 24g • % Daily Value: Vitamin A 22%; Vitamin C 18%; Calcium 6%; Iron 24% • Exchanges: 1 Starch, 1 Vegetable, 2 1/2 Lean Meat • Carbohydrate Choices: 1

together time

Have a chili feast! Set out bowls of your favorite toppings such as shredded Cheddar cheese, chopped onion, sour cream, guacamole and pickled sliced jalapeño chilies.

Southwestern Pot Roast

8 SERVINGS PREP: 15 MIN COOK: 10 HR

8 small red potatoes, cut in half

3-pound beef arm roast, trimmed of fat

1 pound baby-cut carrots

2 tablespoons all-purpose flour

1 jar (16 ounces) salsa

1. Place potatoes in 3 1/2- to 4-quart slow cooker. Place beef on potatoes; arrange carrots around beef. Sprinkle with flour. Pour salsa over all.
2. Cover and cook on low heat setting 8 to 10 hours.
3. Remove beef from cooker; place on cutting board. Pull beef into serving pieces, using 2 forks. To serve, spoon sauce over beef and vegetables.

1 SERVING: Calories 310 (Calories from Fat 70); Fat 8g (Saturated 3g); Cholesterol 65mg; Sodium 260mg; Carbohydrate 33g (Dietary Fiber 5g); Protein 27g • % Daily Value: Vitamin A 100%; Vitamin C 20%; Calcium 4%; Iron 22% • Exchanges: 2 Starch, 1 Vegetable, 3 Very Lean Meat, 1/2 Fat • Carbohydrate Choices: 2

together time

Learn to say "thank you" in another language. Grazie, gracias, merci. Teaching your kids how to say thank you in other languages is fun and encourages cultural curiosity and good manners. Maybe they'll remember to say grazie more often.

Southwestern Pot Roast

Fresh Vegetable, Beef and Barley Soup

8 SERVINGS PREP: 20 MIN COOK: 9 HR

1 1/2 pounds beef stew meat

1 small bell pepper, chopped (1/2 cup)

3/4 cup 1-inch pieces fresh green beans or frozen (thawed) cut green beans

3/4 cup chopped onion

2/3 cup fresh or frozen whole kernel corn

2/3 cup uncooked barley

1 1/2 cups water

1 teaspoon salt

1 teaspoon chopped fresh or 1/2 teaspoon dried thyme leaves

1/4 teaspoon pepper

2 cans (14 ounces each) beef broth

2 cans (14 1/2 ounces each) diced tomatoes with garlic, undrained

1 can (8 ounces) tomato sauce

1. Mix all ingredients in 3 1/2- to 6-quart slow cooker.

2. Cover and cook on low heat setting 8 to 9 hours.

1 SERVING: Calories 290 (Calories from Fat 100); Fat 11g (Saturated 4g); Cholesterol 50mg; Sodium 1140mg; Carbohydrate 25g (Dietary Fiber 5g); Protein 22g • % Daily Value: Vitamin A 14%; Vitamin C 24%; Calcium 6%; Iron 18% • Exchanges: 1 Starch, 1 Vegetable, 2 1/2 Medium-Fat Meat • Carbohydrate Choices: 1 1/2

together time

Serve your soup in edible bowls, and the family will have fun nibbling on the bread. Here's how you do it: Slice a thin layer off the tops of large hard rolls, and hollow them out, leaving a 1/2-inch-thick wall. Fill with soup and enjoy!

Honey Barbecue Pork Roast with Carrots and Corn

8 SERVINGS PREP: 15 MIN COOK: 10 HR 20 MIN

3-pound pork boneless shoulder roast, trimmed of fat

1 bag (1 pound) baby-cut carrots

1/2 cup barbecue sauce

1/4 cup honey

3 tablespoons balsamic vinegar

1 teaspoon seasoned salt

2/3 cup barbecue sauce

1/4 cup all-purpose flour

1 cup frozen whole kernel corn

1. Place pork in 3 1/2- to 4-quart slow cooker. Arrange carrots around and on top of pork. Mix 1/2 cup barbecue sauce, the honey, vinegar and seasoned salt in small bowl; pour over pork and carrots.
2. Cover and cook on low heat setting 8 to 10 hours.
3. Remove pork and carrots from cooker; place on serving platter and cover to keep warm. Mix 2/3 cup barbecue sauce and the flour; gradually stir into juices in cooker. Increase heat setting to high. Cover and cook about 15 minutes, stirring occasionally, until thickened.
4. Stir corn into mixture in cooker. Cover and cook 5 minutes longer. Serve sauce over pork and carrots.

1 SERVING: Calories 600 (Calories from Fat 250); Fat 27g (Saturated 10g); Cholesterol 145mg; Sodium 550mg; Carbohydrate 36g (Dietary Fiber 3g); Protein 51g • % Daily Value: Vitamin A 100%; Vitamin C 8%; Calcium 4%; Iron 14% • Exchanges: 2 Starch, 1 Vegetable, 5 1/2 Medium-Fat Meat • Carbohydrate Choices: 2 1/2

together time

Invite Grandma or a grandma-substitute who enjoys cooking and baking to have a fun day in the kitchen with the kids. Together, look through cookbooks and decide what recipes the kids would like to try.

Spicy Pork Tacos

12 TACOS   PREP: 5 MIN   COOK: 9 HR

2-pound pork boneless center loin roast, cut into 4 × 1/2-inch strips

2 teaspoons ground red chilies

1/2 teaspoon red pepper sauce

1/4 teaspoon ground coriander

1 can (14 1/2 ounces) diced tomatoes, drained

1 can (4 1/2 ounces) chopped green chiles, undrained

12 taco or tostada shells, warmed if desired

3/4 cup shredded Cheddar cheese (3 ounces)

1 1/2 cups shredded lettuce

1. Mix pork, red chilies, red pepper sauce, coriander, tomatoes and green chiles in 3 1/2- to 4-quart slow cooker.
2. Cover and cook on low heat setting 8 to 9 hours.
3. Spoon about 1/3 cup pork mixture into each taco shell, using slotted spoon. Top with cheese and lettuce.

2 TACOS: Calories 450 (Calories from Fat 205); Fat 23g (Saturated 8g); Cholesterol 110mg; Sodium 420mg; Carbohydrate 21g (Dietary Fiber 3g); Protein 40g • % Daily Value: Vitamin A 12%; Vitamin C 14%; Calcium 14%; Iron 14% • Exchanges: 1 Starch, 1 Vegetable, 5 Lean Meat, 1 1/2 Fat • Carbohydrate Choices: 1 1/2

together time

Start a vacation discussion over dinner tonight, and make a list of the places you'd like to visit the next time you take a trip. Post the list on your refrigerator, and add to it as other ideas come up.

Spicy Pork Tacos

Mexican Pork

4 SERVINGS PREP: 5 MIN COOK: 8 HR 5 MIN

1-pound pork boneless loin roast, cut into 1-inch pieces

1 jar (20 ounces) salsa

1 can (4 1/2 ounces) chopped green chiles, drained

1 can (15 to 16 ounces) pinto beans or black beans, rinsed and drained

1 cup shredded Cheddar or Monterey Jack cheese (4 ounces), if desired

Assorted serve-withs (such as hot cooked rice, Spanish rice or tortilla chips or with guacamole or chopped avocado, sour cream, chopped tomato or chopped cilantro), if desired

1. Mix pork, salsa and chilies in 3 1/2- to 4-quart slow cooker.
2. Cover and cook on low heat setting 6 to 8 hours.
3. Stir in beans. Cover and cook about 5 minutes or until hot. Sprinkle with cheese. Serve with desired serve-withs.

1 SERVING: Calories 345 (Calories from Fat 90); Fat 10g (Saturated 3g); Cholesterol 70mg; Sodium 1030mg; Carbohydrate 37g (Dietary Fiber 10g); Protein 37g • % Daily Value: Vitamin A 26%; Vitamin C 34%; Calcium 12%; Iron 30% • Exchanges: 2 Starch, 4 Very Lean Meat, 1 Vegetable, 1/2 Fat • Carbohydrate Choices: 2 1/2

together time

Ask the kids what foods or what vegetables they would like to eat for a meal—it can make a big difference in getting them to try new foods and in making them feel special and important.

Winter Vegetable Stew

4 SERVINGS PREP: 20 MIN COOK: 10 HR 20 MIN

1 can (28 ounces) Italian-style plum tomatoes

4 medium red potatoes, cut into 1/2-inch pieces

4 medium stalks celery, cut into 1/2-inch pieces (2 cups)

3 medium carrots, cut into 1/2-inch pieces (1 1/2 cups)

2 medium parsnips, peeled and cut into 1/2-inch pieces

2 medium leeks, cut into 1/2-inch pieces

1 can (14 ounces) vegetable or chicken broth

1/2 teaspoon salt

1/2 teaspoon dried thyme leaves

1/2 teaspoon dried rosemary leaves

3 tablespoons cornstarch

3 tablespoons cold water

1. Drain tomatoes, reserving liquid. Cut up tomatoes. Mix tomatoes, tomato liquid and remaining ingredients except cornstarch and cold water in 4- to 5-quart slow cooker.
2. Cover and cook on low heat setting 8 to 10 hours.
3. Mix cornstarch and cold water; gradually stir into stew until blended. Increase heat setting to high. Cover and cook about 20 minutes, stirring occasionally, until thickened.

1 SERVING: Calories 130 (Calories from Fat 10); Fat 1g (Saturated 0g); Cholesterol 0mg; Sodium 560mg; Carbohydrate 31g (Dietary Fiber 5g); Protein 4g • % Daily Value: Vitamin A 26%; Vitamin C 26%; Calcium 6%; Iron 10% • Exchanges: 1/2 Starch, 4 Vegetable • Carbohydrate Choices: 2

together time

Have an indoor treasure hunt! Parents hide an object, and the kids look for it. Things to hide could be small stuffed animals, large buttons or other things around the house. Now it's the kids' turn to hide something for the parents to hunt for.

Chapter 5

I Did It!

In this chapter, the kids do the cooking while Mom and Dad take it easy. Be on the lookout, though, they may need just a little help cutting veggies, browning meat or draining pasta. But don't be tempted to help too much; let them do as much as possible, and they'll feel a tremendous sense of accomplishment. Who knows? It could just become a habit!

Cheesy Chicken Strips (page 128)

Cheesy Chicken Strips

Photo on page 127

4 SERVINGS   PREP: 10 MIN   BAKE: 12 MIN

1 pound boneless, skinless chicken breast halves or chicken breast tenders (not breaded)

2 cups cheese-flavored crackers, crushed (1 cup)

1/2 cup finely shredded Cheddar cheese (2 ounces)

1 egg

Barbecue sauce, ketchup or ranch dressing, if desired

1. Heat oven to 400°. Spray jelly roll pan, 15 1/2 × 10 1/2 × 1 inch, with cooking spray. If using chicken breast halves, cut chicken lengthwise into 1/2-inch strips.
2. Mix crushed crackers and cheese in large resealable plastic food-storage bag. Beat egg in large bowl. Add chicken strips to egg and toss to coat. Remove chicken from egg, allowing excess to drip off into bowl; place chicken in bag of cracker mixture. Seal bag and shake to coat evenly with cracker mixture. Place chicken strips in single layer in pan.
3. Bake uncovered 10 to 12 minutes or until no longer pink in center. Serve with barbecue sauce.

1 SERVING: Calories 355 (Calories from Fat 155); Fat 17g (Saturated 7g); Cholesterol 130mg; Sodium 7mg; Carbohydrate 19g (Dietary Fiber 1g); Protein 34g • % Daily Value: Vitamin A 4%; Vitamin C 0%; Calcium 14%; Iron 14% • Exchanges: 1 Starch, 5 Lean Meat • Carbohydrate Choices: 1

together time

Creatively crush the crackers for the chicken in a sturdy, sealed plastic food-storage bag. Give the bag to the kids to let them crush the crackers with a play rolling pin or the back of a pan, or let them roll their tiny cars over the crackers.

Super-Easy Chicken Manicotti

Cowboy Chicken and Beans

6 SERVINGS   PREP: 5 MIN   BAKE: 40 MIN

2 cups shredded fully cooked chicken, beef or pork in barbecue sauce (from 20-ounce tub)

1 can (15 to 16 ounces) garbanzo beans, rinsed and drained

1 can (15 to 16 ounces) lima beans, rinsed and drained

1 can (15 to 16 ounces) kidney beans, rinsed and drained

1 cup shredded Cheddar cheese (4 ounces)

1. Heat oven to 350°. Spray 2-quart casserole with cooking spray. Mix chicken and beans in casserole.
2. Bake uncovered 30 to 35 minutes or until hot and bubbly. Sprinkle with cheese. Bake about 5 minutes or until cheese is melted.

1 SERVING: Calories 400 (Calories from Fat 135); Fat 15g (Saturated 6g); Cholesterol 75mg; Sodium 910mg; Carbohydrate 43g (Dietary Fiber 11g); Protein 34g • % Daily Value: Vitamin A 6%; Vitamin C 4%; Calcium 16%; Iron 30% • Exchanges: 2 1/2 Starch, 3 1/2 Lean Meat, 1 Vegetable • Carbohydrate Choices: 3

together time

Play with your food! Make a zany zucchini cowboy head centerpiece. Slice off one end of a large zucchini, and stand it on a plate. Decorate the top to look like a face, attaching food pieces such as carrot slices, raisins and grapes with toothpicks. Top it off with toy hat and bandana!

Saturday Night Supper

4 SERVINGS PREP: 20 MIN BAKE: 30 MIN

3/4 cup uncooked small pasta shells or elbow macaroni

1 pound ground chicken or turkey

2 cups frozen mixed vegetables (from 1-pound bag)

1 can (15 ounces) Italian-style tomato sauce

3/4 teaspoon garlic salt

1/4 teaspoon pepper

1/4 cup shredded Parmesan cheese

1. Heat oven to 400°. Cook pasta as directed on package. While pasta is cooking, cook chicken in 10-inch skillet over medium heat about 10 minutes, stirring occasionally, until no longer pink; drain.
2. Spoon chicken into ungreased 2-quart casserole. Stir in frozen vegetables, tomato sauce, pasta, garlic salt and pepper.
3. Cover and bake about 30 minutes or until vegetables are tender. Stir; sprinkle with cheese.

1 SERVING: **Calories 370 (Calories from Fat 120); Fat 13g (Saturated 3g); Cholesterol 80mg; Sodium 960mg; Carbohydrate 38g (Dietary Fiber 4g); Protein 32g • % Daily Value: Vitamin A 42%; Vitamin C 28%; Calcium 14%; Iron 16% • Exchanges: 2 Starch, 3 Lean Meat, 2 Vegetable • Carbohydrate Choices: 2 1/2**

together time

Turn it into a game! If kids don't want to eat their vegetables, make eating them more fun by slicing carrot "coins," creating broccoli and cauliflower "trees" or turning celery sticks into "logs" filled with peanut butter.

family fun

TGIF NIGHT

In your house, TGIF can stand for Thank Goodness It's Family Night, any night of the week or weekend. Get the whole family involved to quickly get dinner on the table together. Or parents can take a break while the kids pick a very easy menu and even do the cooking. Kids will find easy-to-follow directions for their favorites that they can make by themselves.

Menu

Easy Fish and Veggie Packets (page 38)

Alphabet Breadstick Dunkers (at right)

Fruit and Cheese 'Bobs (at right)

Puffy Popcorn Balls (at right)

Corbis Digital Stock

Alphabet Breadstick Dunkers

Heat oven to 375°. Unroll 1 can (11 ounces) **refrigerated breadsticks** dough; separate at perforations to form 12 strips. Shape strips of dough into desired letters of the alphabet on ungreased cookie sheet. Bake 13 to 15 minutes or until golden brown. Meanwhile, heat 1 cup **pizza or pasta sauce** in small saucepan over medium heat until hot. Dip breadsticks into warm pizza sauce.

Fruit and Cheese 'Bobs

Cut 8 cubes from 1/2 block (4 ounces) **Cheddar cheese** and 8 cubes from 1 **honeydew melon or cantaloupe**. Thread 2 cheese cubes and 2 melon cubes alternately on each of four 10-inch bamboo skewers. Add 1 **strawberry** to each end of skewer.

Puffy Popcorn Balls

Heat 1 bag (10 ounces) **large marshmallows** and 1/4 cup **butter** in large saucepan over medium heat, stirring constantly, just until marshmallows are melted; remove from heat. Add 8 cups **popped popcorn**; stir until evenly coated. Cool 5 minutes. Using buttered hands, shape mixture by cupfuls into balls.

More TGIF Ideas

Thank goodness there are lots of other easy dishes to try. Why not make these instead?

Easy Beans and Franks Soup (page 28)
Chili-Cheese Hash Browns (page 57)
Family Heroes (page 82)
Pizza Burgers (page 146)

helping is fun

Mom or Dad

- Rests
- Is on hand for questions
- Rests some more!

The Kids

- Make Easy Fish and Veggie Packets
- Make Alphabet Breadstick Dunkers
- Place fruit and cheese on skewers

together time

Pop popcorn after dinner and mix together with marshmallow mixture. For a fun way to decorate, sprinkle with edible glitter.

Think of an activity everyone can do together. Maybe it's as simple as playing cards or your favorite board game. Interacting with your kids in enjoyable activities is a great way to stay in touch!

Plan a cozy fireside supper. Pull chairs and TV trays close to the hearth, or spread a blanket on the floor, picnic style, and bask in the warmth.

Declare a video night. Pick a favorite movie or any movie that you all can enjoy together. How about a classic like *Harvey*, the story of an imaginary friend, or *Fly Away Home*, about a great adventure in nature? Have a big bowl of popcorn, just like at the movies.

Kid-Pleasin' Chili

8 SERVINGS (ABOUT 9 CUPS) PREP: 5 MIN COOK: 40 MIN

2 pounds ground beef

2 cans (15 to 16 ounces each) kidney beans, rinsed and drained

2 cans (10 3/4 ounces each) condensed tomato soup

2 soup cans water

2 tablespoons instant minced onion

4 to 6 teaspoons chili powder

Shredded Cheddar cheese or tiny fish-shaped crackers, if desired

1. Cook beef in 4-quart Dutch oven over medium heat about 10 minutes, stirring occasionally, until brown; drain.
2. Stir remaining ingredients except cheese into beef. Heat to boiling, reduce heat. Cover and simmer 30 minutes, stirring occasionally. Sprinkle with cheese.

1 SERVING: Calories 400 (Calories from Fat 160); Fat 18g (Saturated 7g); Cholesterol 65mg; Sodium 770mg; Carbohydrate 37g (Dietary Fiber 8g); Protein 31g • % Daily Value: Vitamin A 16%; Vitamin C 10%; Calcium 4%; Iron 30% • Exchanges: 2 Starch, 3 Medium-Fat Meat, 1 Vegetable • Carbohydrate Choices: 2 1/2

together time

Watch the snowflakes fall. Catch some flakes on your hand and try to see if every one really is different from the others. If the weather cooperates, build a snowman or other snow creature together.

Impossibly Easy Taco Pie

6 SERVINGS PREP: 10 MIN COOK: 10 MIN BAKE: 35 MIN STAND: 5 MIN

1 pound ground beef

1 medium onion, chopped (1/2 cup)

1 envelope (1.25 ounces) taco seasoning mix

1 can (4 1/2 ounces) chopped green chiles, drained

1 1/4 cups milk

3 eggs

3/4 cup Original Bisquick mix

1 cup shredded Colby-Monterey Jack or Cheddar cheese (4 ounces)

1. Heat oven to 400°. Spray pie plate, 10 × 1 1/2 inches, with cooking spray. Cook beef and onion in 10-inch skillet over medium heat about 10 minutes, stirring occasionally, until beef is brown; drain.
2. Stir taco seasoning mix (dry) into beef. Spread beef mixture in pie plate. Top with chiles. Stir milk, eggs and Bisquick mix in small bowl with fork until blended; pour into pie plate.
3. Bake 25 minutes. Sprinkle with cheese. Bake 8 to 10 minutes or until knife inserted in center comes out clean. Let stand 5 minutes before cutting.

1 SERVING: Calories 365 (Calories from Fat 200); Fat 22g (Saturated 10g); Cholesterol 175mg; Sodium 660mg; Carbohydrate 18g (Dietary Fiber 1g); Protein 25g • % Daily Value: Vitamin A 20%; Vitamin C 2%; Calcium 26%; Iron 11% • Exchanges: 1 Starch, 3 Lean Meat, 2 1/2 Fat • Carbohydrate Choices: 1

together time

Volunteer together to help a neighbor rake leaves or mow the lawn. Or lend a hand as a family at a charity where meals are served or where food is packed for hungry children.

Ravioli Supper Soup

4 SERVINGS PREP: 5 MIN COOK: 25 MIN STAND: 5 MIN

1 pound ground beef

1 package (7.8 ounces) ravioli and cheese skillet-dinner mix for hamburger

6 cups hot water

1 can (14 1/2 ounces) diced tomatoes, undrained

1 package (10 ounces) frozen mixed vegetables, thawed and drained

1/4 cup finely chopped onion or 2 tablespoons instant minced onion

2 cloves garlic, finely chopped

1 cup small curd creamed cottage cheese

Shredded Parmesan cheese, if desired

1. Cook beef in 4-quart Dutch oven over medium heat about 10 minutes, stirring occasionally, until brown; drain.
2. Stir uncooked Pasta and Sauce Mix from dinner mix, water, tomatoes, vegetables, onion and garlic into beef. Heat to boiling, stirring occasionally; reduce heat. Cover and simmer about 15 minutes, stirring occasionally, until pasta is tender.
3. Remove from heat; stir in cottage cheese. Let stand about 5 minutes or until desired consistency. Serve with Parmesan cheese.

1 SERVING: Calories 520 (Calories from Fat 180); Fat 20g (Saturated 9g); Cholesterol 70mg; Sodium 1440mg; Carbohydrate 55g (Dietary Fiber 5g); Protein 35g • % Daily Value: Vitamin A 52%; Vitamin C 32%; Calcium 18%; Iron 20% • Exchanges: 3 Starch, 3 Medium-Fat Meat, 2 Vegetable • Carbohydrate Choices: 3 1/2

together time

Write down topics on scraps of paper, and place in a bowl. Have each person choose a piece of paper from the bowl, and let them talk about the subject. Topics might include Best Part of the Day, Favorite Memory or Most Embarrassing Moment.

Ravioli Supper Soup

Beef 'n Veggie Soup with Mozzarella

8 SERVINGS PREP: 10 MIN COOK: 20 MIN

1 pound ground beef

1 large onion, chopped (1 cup)

1 can (14 1/2 ounces) diced tomatoes with green pepper, celery and onions, undrained

4 cups beef broth

1 1/2 teaspoons Italian seasoning

1/4 teaspoon pepper

1 package (10 ounces) frozen mixed vegetables

1 cup shredded mozzarella cheese (4 ounces)

1. Cook beef and onion in 4-quart Dutch oven over medium-high heat about 10 minutes, stirring occasionally, until beef is brown; drain.
2. Stir remaining ingredients except cheese into beef. Heat to boiling; reduce heat. Simmer uncovered 6 to 8 minutes, stirring occasionally, until vegetables are tender.
3. Sprinkle about 2 tablespoons cheese in each of 8 soup bowls. Fill bowls with soup.

1 SERVING: Calories 185 (Calories from Fat 100); Fat 11g (Saturated 5g); Cholesterol 40mg; Sodium 1050mg; Carbohydrate 8g (Dietary Fiber 2g); Protein 16g • % Daily Value: Vitamin A 24%; Vitamin C 16%; Calcium 14%; Iron 8% • Exchanges: 2 Medium-Fat Meat, 2 Vegetable • Carbohydrate Choices: 1/2

together time

Start a kitchen garden by buying and sprouting alfalfa seeds, mung beans or dry peas. Or plant seeds for chives or other herbs in a small planter to keep by the kitchen window.

Beef-Barley Stew

6 SERVINGS   PREP: 12 MIN   BAKE: 1 HR 10 MIN

1 pound extra-lean ground beef

1 medium onion, chopped (1/2 cup)

2 cups beef broth

2/3 cup uncooked barley

2 teaspoons chopped fresh or 1/2 teaspoon dried oregano leaves

1/4 teaspoon salt

1/4 teaspoon pepper

1 can (14 1/2 ounces) whole tomatoes, undrained

1 can (8 ounces) sliced water chestnuts, undrained

1 package (10 ounces) frozen mixed vegetables

1. Heat oven to 350°. Spray 10-inch nonstick skillet with cooking spray; heat over medium heat. Cook beef and onion in skillet about 10 minutes, stirring occasionally, until beef is brown; drain.
2. Mix beef mixture and remaining ingredients except frozen vegetables in ungreased 3-quart casserole, breaking up tomatoes.
3. Cover and bake 30 minutes. Stir in frozen vegetables. Cover and bake 30 to 40 minutes longer or until barley is tender.

1 SERVING: Calories 275 (Calories from Fat 80); Fat 9g (Saturated 3g); Cholesterol 45mg; Sodium 600mg; Carbohydrate 29g (Dietary Fiber 7g); Protein 24g • % Daily Value: Vitamin A 32%; Vitamin C 24%; Calcium 6%; Iron 18% • Exchanges: 2 Starch, 2 Lean Meat • Carbohydrate Choices: 2

together time

Pick a summer day for the family to spend at a pick-your-own strawberry or blueberry garden. Or pick a fall day for a trip to an apple orchard or a pumpkin farm. Some of the farms have animals to pet and crafts to shop for as well as lots of fresh air!

Cheesy Italian Ravioli

6 SERVINGS PREP: 15 MIN BAKE: 25 MIN

1/2 pound ground beef

1/2 pound bulk Italian sausage

1 container (15 ounces) refrigerated marinara sauce

1 cup sliced fresh mushrooms

1 can (14 1/2 ounces) diced tomatoes with Italian seasonings, undrained

1 package (9 ounces) refrigerated cheese-filled ravioli

1 cup shredded mozzarella cheese or pizza cheese blend (4 ounces)

1. Heat oven to 375°. Cook beef and sausage in 10-inch skillet over medium heat about 10 minutes, stirring occasionally, until brown; drain.
2. Stir marinara sauce, mushrooms and tomatoes into beef mixture. Pour half of sauce mixture into ungreased rectangular baking dish, 11 × 7 × 1 1/2 inches. Arrange ravioli in sauce in dish. Pour remaining sauce mixture over ravioli. Sprinkle with cheese.
3. Bake uncovered 20 to 25 minutes or until ravioli is tender and mixture is hot.

1 SERVING: Calories 460 (Calories from Fat 235); Fat 26g (Saturated 10g); Cholesterol 105mg; Sodium 1020mg; Carbohydrate 30g (Dietary Fiber 3g); Protein 27g • % Daily Value: Vitamin A 22%; Vitamin C 20%; Calcium 26%; Iron 16% • Exchanges: 2 Starch, 3 Medium-Fat Meat, 2 Fat • Carbohydrate Choices: 2

together time

Get out the bubbles and bubble makers, and have a blast blowing bubbles. If you like to blow really large ones, you may want to take this game outside. No bubbles or makers? Use dishwashing detergent and a bent hanger to make very large bubbles.

Cheeseburger Pasta Toss

6 SERVINGS   PREP: 5 MIN   COOK: 15 MIN

2 cups uncooked wagon wheel or tricolored rotini pasta (4 ounces)

1 pound ground beef

1 large onion, sliced or chopped (1 cup)

1 jar (8 ounces) process sharp Cheddar cheese spread

1/2 cup milk

1/2 teaspoon garlic salt

1 large tomato, chopped (1 cup)

1/2 cup shredded Cheddar cheese (2 ounces)

1. Cook and drain pasta as directed on package.
2. While pasta is cooking, cook beef and onion in 10-inch skillet over medium-high heat about 10 minutes, stirring occasionally, until beef is brown; drain.
3. Reduce heat to medium. Stir cheese spread, milk and garlic salt into beef; continue stirring until cheese is melted and mixture is well blended. Stir in pasta and tomato. Sprinkle with Cheddar cheese; cover and heat 2 to 3 minutes or until cheese is melted.

1 SERVING: Calories 475 (Calories from Fat 205); Fat 23g (Saturated 12g); Cholesterol 85mg; Sodium 760mg; Carbohydrate 39g (Dietary Fiber 2g); Protein 29g • % Daily Value: Vitamin A 18%; Vitamin C 6%; Calcium 26%; Iron 16% • Exchanges: 2 1/2 Starch, 3 Medium-Fat Meat, 1 Fat • Carbohydrate Choices: 2 1/2

together time

Give each family member a disposable camera to shoot and record impressions of the family. Collect the prints in an album, and have each family member write captions. You'll have an invaluable memory collection!

Rigatoni Pizza Stew

4 SERVINGS PREP: 15 MIN COOK: 30 MIN

1 pound Italian sausage links, cut into 1/4-inch slices

1 can (14 1/2 ounces) Italian-style stewed tomatoes, undrained

1 can (14 ounces) beef broth

1 cup water

1/4 cup Italian-style tomato paste

1 medium onion, coarsely chopped (1/2 cup)

2 medium carrots, cut into 1/2-inch slices (1 cup)

1 1/2 cups uncooked rigatoni pasta (4 1/2 ounces)

1 medium zucchini, cut lengthwise in half, then cut crosswise into 1/4-inch slices (2 cups)

1/2 cup shredded mozzarella cheese (2 ounces)

1. Spray 4-quart Dutch oven with cooking spray. Cook sausage in Dutch oven over medium heat about 8 minutes, stirring occasionally, until no longer pink; drain.

2. Stir tomatoes, broth, water, tomato paste, onion and carrots into sausage. Heat to boiling; reduce heat to medium-low. Cook about 10 minutes or until carrots are tender.

3. Stir in pasta and zucchini. Cook 10 to 12 minutes, stirring occasionally, until pasta is tender. Serve topped with cheese.

1 SERVING: Calories 475 (Calories from Fat 225); Fat 25g (Saturated 9g); Cholesterol 70mg; Sodium 1740mg; Carbohydrate 44g (Dietary Fiber 5g); Protein 29g • % Daily Value: Vitamin A 100%; Vitamin C 24%; Calcium 18%; Iron 22% • Exchanges: 2 1/2 Starch, 2 1/2 Medium-Fat Meat, 1 1/2 Vegetable, 1 Fat • Carbohydrate Choices: 3

together time

Let the calendar inspire you to do fun things together. Take a family bike ride during National Bike Month, celebrate National Wildflower Week by looking at wildflowers while going for a walk or read a book together once a week during Get Caught Reading Month.

Rigatoni Pizza Stew

Pizza Burgers

6 BURGERS   PREP: 5 MIN   COOK: 14 MIN

1 pound ground beef

1 medium onion, chopped (1/2 cup)

1 small green bell pepper, chopped (1/2 cup)

1 jar (14 ounces) pepperoni-flavored or regular pizza sauce

1/2 cup sliced ripe olives

6 whole wheat sandwich buns, split

1 cup shredded pizza cheese blend (4 ounces)

1. Cook beef, onion and bell pepper in 10-inch skillet over medium heat about 10 minutes, stirring occasionally, until beef is brown; drain.

2. Stir pizza sauce and olives into beef. Heat to boiling, stirring occasionally.

3. Spoon about 1/2 cup beef mixture on bottom half of each bun. Immediately sprinkle each with 2 or 3 tablespoons of the cheese; add tops of buns. Serve immediately or let stand about 2 minutes until cheese is melted.

1 BURGER: Calories 360 (Calories from Fat 180); Fat 20g (Saturated 7g); Cholesterol 55mg; Sodium 790mg; Carbohydrate 25g (Dietary Fiber 4g); Protein 24g • % Daily Value: Vitamin A 12%; Vitamin C 22%; Calcium 24%; Iron 20% • Exchanges: 1 1/2 Starch, 2 1/2 Medium-Fat Meat, 1/2 Fat • Carbohydrate Choices: 1 1/2

together time

Give your family something to smile about! Let the kids make smiling faces on these burgers with sliced pimiento-stuffed olives, pickle slices and squeezes of ketchup and mustard. Or use whatever you have on hand to make the faces.

Burger and Veggie Packets

5 PACKETS PREP: 15 MIN BAKE: 20 MIN

1 pound extra-lean or diet-lean ground beef

1 tablespoon Worcestershire sauce

1 teaspoon garlic pepper

1/2 teaspoon onion powder

2 cups frozen sugar snap peas, carrots, onions and mushrooms (or other combination)

30 frozen steak fries (from 28-ounce bag)

5 frozen half-ears corn-on-the-cob

1/2 teaspoon garlic pepper

1. Heat oven to 450°. Cut five 18 × 12-inch sheets of aluminum foil. Mix beef, Worcestershire sauce, 1 teaspoon garlic pepper and the onion powder. Shape mixture into 5 patties, about 1/4 inch thick.
2. Place 1 patty on each foil sheet about 2 inches from 12-inch side. Top each with frozen vegetables and steak fries. Place 1 piece of corn next to each patty. Sprinkle 1/2 teaspoon garlic pepper over vegetables. Fold foil over patties and vegetables so edges meet. Seal edges, making tight 1/2-inch fold; fold again. Allow space on sides for circulation and expansion. Place packets on large cookie sheet.
3. Bake 15 to 20 minutes or until patties are no longer pink in center and juice of beef is clear. Place packets on plates. Cut large × across top of each packet; fold back foil.

1 PACKET: Calories 380 (Calories from Fat 135); Fat 15g (Saturated 5g); Cholesterol 50mg; Sodium 450mg; Carbohydrate 34g (Dietary Fiber 4g); Protein 22g • % Daily Value: Vitamin A 64%; Vitamin C 18%; Calcium 2%; Iron 18% • Exchanges: 2 Starch, 1 Vegetable, 2 Medium-Fat Meat, 1 Fat • Carbohydrate Choices: 2

together time

Celebrate a good grade, a great music practice or a winning game by letting the kids prepare dinner by themselves. Cooking a meal from beginning to end makes kids feel more confident and independent. Remember to be on hand for questions.

Chicken-Fried Pork Chops

4 PORK CHOPS PREP: 10 MIN COOK: 8 MIN

- 4 pork boneless loin chops (4 ounces each)
- 1/4 cup all-purpose flour
- 1/2 teaspoon seasoned salt
- 1/4 teaspoon garlic powder
- 2 to 3 tablespoons milk
- 1/2 cup Italian-style dry bread crumbs
- 2 tablespoons vegetable oil

1. To flatten each pork chop, place between 2 pieces of plastic wrap or waxed paper. Working from center, gently pound pork with flat side of meat mallet or rolling pin until about 1/4 inch thick; remove wrap.
2. Mix flour, seasoned salt and garlic powder in shallow bowl. Place milk and bread crumbs in separate shallow bowls. Dip each pork chop into flour mixture, then dip into milk. Coat well with bread crumbs.
3. Heat oil in 12-inch skillet over medium heat. Cook pork chops in oil 6 to 8 minutes, turning once, until pork is browned on outside and slightly pink in center.

1 PORK CHOP: Calories 300 (Calories from Fat 140); Fat 15g (Saturated 4g); Cholesterol 60mg; Sodium 450mg; Carbohydrate 17g (Dietary Fiber 1g); Protein 24g • % Daily Value: Vitamin A 0%; Vitamin C 0%; Calcium 4%; Iron 10% • Exchanges: 1 Starch, 3 Very Lean Meat, 2 1/2 Fat • Carbohydrate Choices: 1

together time

Make it a Classics Night! Serve a classic dinner, such as these pork chops with mashed potatoes and corn, have brownies for dessert, and watch a classic movie such as *Gone with the Wind, Black Beauty* or—a new classic—*Harry Potter*, while munching on classic buttered popcorn.

Hot Dog Casserole

4 SERVINGS PREP: 15 MIN BAKE: 30 MIN

- 1 1/3 cups mashed potato mix (dry)
- 1 1/3 cups water
- 1/3 cup milk
- 2 tablespoons butter or margarine
- 1/2 teaspoon salt
- 1/4 cup sweet pickle relish
- 2 tablespoons mayonnaise or salad dressing
- 1 tablespoon instant minced onion
- 2 teaspoons mustard
- 4 to 6 franks

1. Heat oven to 350°. Make mashed potatoes as directed on package, using water, milk, butter and salt. Stir in relish, mayonnaise, onion and mustard. Spread in ungreased 1-quart casserole.
2. Cut each frank lengthwise in half, then crosswise in half. Insert frank pieces around edge of mashed potatoes.
3. Bake uncovered 25 to 30 minutes or until center is hot.

1 SERVING: Calories 345 (Calories from Fat 225); Fat 25g (Saturated 9g); Cholesterol 40mg; Sodium 1080mg; Carbohydrate 23g (Dietary Fiber 2g); Protein 7g • % Daily Value: Vitamin A 6%; Vitamin C 6%; Calcium 4%; Iron 4% • Exchanges: 1 1/2 Starch, 5 Fat • Carbohydrate Choices: 1 1/2

together time

Dig into those trunks, the back of your closet or other clothes storage areas, and let the kids have fun dressing up in your old clothes. Who knows? You might even find something "new" to wear.

Fish Sticks Marinara

6 SERVINGS PREP: 10 MIN BAKE: 30 MIN

2 packages (10 ounces each) frozen broccoli spears, thawed and drained

1 tablespoon olive or vegetable oil

1/2 teaspoon dried basil leaves

1/2 teaspoon chopped garlic

12 frozen breaded fish sticks

1 container (15 ounces) marinara sauce or 2 cups tomato pasta sauce (any variety)

1/4 cup shredded Parmesan cheese

6 slices (1 ounce each) mozzarella cheese

1. Heat oven to 350°. Arrange broccoli in ungreased square baking dish, 8 × 8 × 2 inches. Drizzle with oil; sprinkle with basil and garlic.
2. Place fish on broccoli. Spoon marinara sauce over fish. Sprinkle with Parmesan cheese. Arrange mozzarella cheese on top.
3. Bake uncovered about 30 minutes or until heated through.

1 SERVING: Calories 315 (Calories from Fat 145); Fat 16g (Saturated 5g); Cholesterol 30mg; Sodium 760mg; Carbohydrate 28g (Dietary Fiber 4g); Protein 18g • % Daily Value: Vitamin A 42%; Vitamin C 38%; Calcium 38%; Iron 8% • Exchanges: 1 Starch, 1 High-Fat Meat, 3 Vegetable, 1 Fat • Carbohydrate Choices: 2

together time

Say Cheese! To make a fun "kid-rific" presentation, cut shapes from the mozzarella cheese slices with small cookie cutters and arrange on the casserole for the last 5 minutes of baking.

Fish Sticks Marinara

Tuna Noodle Casserole

5 SERVINGS PREP: 10 MIN BAKE: 35 MIN STAND: 5 MIN

1 package (8.25 ounces) creamy pasta skillet-dinner mix for tuna

2 1/2 cups boiling water

1/4 cup milk

1 can (6 ounces) tuna, drained

4 medium green onions, finely chopped (1/4 cup)

1 package (10 ounces) frozen green peas, rinsed and drained

1 can (10 3/4 ounces) condensed cream of mushroom soup

1 cup crushed sour cream–and–chive potato chips or tiny fish-shaped crackers

1. Heat oven to 425°. Mix uncooked Pasta and Sauce Mix from dinner mix and remaining ingredients except potato chips in ungreased 2-quart round casserole.

2. Cover and bake 30 minutes. Stir; sprinkle with potato chips. Bake uncovered 5 minutes longer. Let stand 5 minutes before serving.

1 SERVING: Calories 405 (Calories from Fat 155); Fat 17g (Saturated 4g); Cholesterol 40mg; Sodium 1440mg; Carbohydrate 49g (Dietary Fiber 5g); Protein 19g • % Daily Value: Vitamin A 20%; Vitamin C 8%; Calcium 14%; Iron 18% • Exchanges: 3 Starch, 1 1/2 Medium-Fat Meat, 1 Fat • Carbohydrate Choices: 3

together time

Pick a timeless book such as Charlotte's Web; A Wrinkle in Time; The Lion, the Witch and the Wardrobe; The Pagemaster; or Harry Potter and the Sorcerer's Stone, and take turns reading a chapter out loud once a week. Or have older kids read the books on their own, then discuss as a family during dinner.

Stacked Enchilada Bake

6 SERVINGS PREP: 10 MIN BAKE: 20 MIN

12 corn tortillas (5 or 6 inches in diameter), torn into bite-size pieces

2 cans (15 to 16 ounces each) chili beans in sauce, undrained

1 can (10 ounces) enchilada sauce

1 1/2 cups shredded Monterey Jack cheese (6 ounces)

3 medium green onions, sliced (3 tablespoons)

1. Heat oven to 400°. Spray 2-quart casserole with cooking spray.
2. Place half of the tortilla pieces in casserole; top with 1 can of beans. Repeat layers. Pour enchilada sauce oven beans and tortilla pieces. Sprinkle with cheese and onions.
3. Bake uncovered about 20 minutes or until bubbly around edge.

1 SERVING: Calories 370 (Calories from Fat 100); Fat 11g (Saturated 6g); Cholesterol 25mg; Sodium 1500mg; Carbohydrate 50g (Dietary Fiber 9g); Protein 18g • % Daily Value: Vitamin A 24%; Vitamin C 20%; Calcium 36%; Iron 22% • Exchanges: 3 Starch, 1 Vegetable, 1 Lean Meat, 1 Fat • Carbohydrate Choices: 3

together time

Come up with a list of fun things to do on a rainy day. Keep the list handy so you can add to it, and pick up any needed supplies when you think of it. On the next rainy day, take out your list and decide what to do. After the rain, keep everyone on the alert for a single or double rainbow.

Mexican Macaroni and Cheese

4 SERVINGS PREP: 10 MIN COOK: 5 MIN

2 cups uncooked radiatore (nugget) pasta (6 ounces)

1 1/2 cups shredded Colby-Monterey Jack cheese (6 ounces)

1/4 cup sliced ripe olives

1/2 cup milk

1/2 teaspoon salt

1 small red bell pepper, chopped (1/2 cup)

1 can (4 1/2 ounces) chopped green chiles, drained

1. Cook and drain pasta as directed on package.

2. Stir remaining ingredients into pasta. Cook over low heat about 5 minutes, stirring occasionally, until cheese is melted and sauce is hot.

1 SERVING: **Calories 365 (Calories from Fat 145); Fat 16g (Saturated 9g); Cholesterol 45mg; Sodium 750mg; Carbohydrate 38g (Dietary Fiber 3g); Protein 17g • % Daily Value: Vitamin A 36%; Vitamin C 34%; Calcium 36%; Iron 14% • Exchanges: 2 1/2 Starch, 1 High-Fat Meat, 1 1/2 Fat • Carbohydrate Choices: 2 1/2**

together time

Learn a few words or phrases in another language. "Hola, cómo está?" (OH-la, como es-TAH) and "Me llamo ____" (May YAM-oh) mean "Hello, how are you?" and "My name is ____" in Spanish. Go around the table and have everyone repeat the new words.

Mexican Macaroni and Cheese

Chapter 6

Sunday Night Dinners

Take a break from the rush-hour workweek to spend relaxed time cooking dinner on Sundays. Some weekends, you may feel like going all out; other weeks, you may not feel like cooking at all—so let your partner or the kids take over. Whatever your mood, here are recipe choices for the amount of time *you* want to spend cooking.

Sausage and Pizza Bake (page 158)

Sausage and Pizza Bake

Photo on page 157

6 SERVINGS PREP: 15 MIN BAKE: 35 MIN

2 cups uncooked rotini pasta (6 ounces)

1 pound bulk Italian sausage

1 medium onion, chopped (1/2 cup)

1 small bell pepper, chopped (1/2 cup)

1/4 cup water

4 ounces sliced Canadian-style bacon, cut into fourths

1 jar or can (14 or 15 ounces) pizza sauce

1 can (4 ounces) sliced mushrooms, drained

3/4 cup shredded pizza cheese blend (3 ounces)

1. Heat oven to 350°. Spray 3-quart casserole with cooking spray. Cook and drain pasta in 3-quart saucepan as directed on package. Return drained pasta to saucepan.
2. While pasta is cooking, cook sausage and onion in 10-inch skillet over medium heat about 8 minutes, stirring occasionally, until sausage is no longer pink; drain. Stir sausage mixture, bell pepper, water, bacon, pizza sauce and mushrooms into drained pasta. Spoon pasta mixture into casserole. Sprinkle with cheese.
3. Cover and bake 30 to 35 minutes or until hot and cheese is melted.

1 SERVING: **Calories 405 (Calories from Fat 190); Fat 21g (Saturated 7g); Cholesterol 55mg; Sodium 1070mg; Carbohydrate 32g (Dietary Fiber 3g); Protein 22g • % Daily Value: Vitamin A 10%; Vitamin C 22%; Calcium 16%; Iron 14% • Exchanges: 2 Starch, 2 High-Fat Meat, 1 Fat • Carbohydrate Choices: 2**

together time

Dine by candlelight. Once dinner is served, turn off all the lights in the house and eat by candlelight. Share your favorite spooky (or other) stories during the meal.

Ravioli-Sausage Lasagna

8 SERVINGS PREP: 15 MIN BAKE: 1 HR STAND: 10 MIN

1 1/4 pounds bulk Italian sausage

1 jar (26 to 28 ounces) tomato pasta sauce (any variety)

1 package (25 to 27 1/2 ounces) frozen cheese-filled ravioli

2 1/2 cups shredded mozzarella cheese (10 ounces)

2 tablespoons grated Parmesan cheese

1. Heat oven to 350°. Cook sausage in 10-inch skillet over medium heat, about 8 minutes, stirring occasionally, until no longer pink; drain.
2. Spread 1/2 cup of the pasta sauce in ungreased rectangular pan, 13 × 9 × 2 inches. Arrange single layer of frozen ravioli over sauce; pour 1 cup pasta sauce evenly over ravioli. Sprinkle evenly with 1 1/2 cups sausage and 1 cup of the mozzarella cheese. Repeat layers with remaining ravioli, pasta sauce and sausage.
3. Cover with aluminum foil and bake 45 minutes. Remove foil; sprinkle with remaining 1 1/2 cups mozzarella and the Parmesan cheese. Bake about 15 minutes or until cheese is melted and lasagna is hot in center. Let stand 10 minutes before cutting.

1 SERVING: Calories 540 (Calories from Fat 270); Fat 30g (Saturated 13g); Cholesterol 150mg; Sodium 1880mg; Carbohydrate 35g (Dietary Fiber 2g); Protein 32g • % Daily Value: Vitamin A 22%; Vitamin C 12%; Calcium 48%; Iron 14% • Exchanges: 2 Starch, 3 1/2 High-Fat Meat, 1 Vegetable, 2 Fat • Carbohydrate Choices: 2

together time

Share silly or funny stories during dinner. Kids love hearing about the words or sounds they made when they were first beginning to talk or the funny things that happened to you when you were growing up.

Grilled Sausage and Cheddar Potato Packets

4 PACKETS PREP: 10 MIN GRILL: 25 MIN

3/4 cup process Cheddar cheese sauce (from 16-ounce jar)

1/2 cup shredded reduced-fat Cheddar cheese (2 ounces)

2 cups frozen stir-fry bell peppers and onions (from 1-pound bag)

2 cups refrigerated diced potatoes with onions (from 20-ounce bag)

1 pound fully cooked turkey smoked sausage, cut into 1 1/2-inch pieces

1. Heat coals or gas grill for direct heat. Spray four 18 × 12-inch sheets of heavy-duty aluminum foil with cooking spray.
2. Mix cheese sauce and shredded cheese in medium bowl. Stir in stir-fry vegetables and potatoes. Arrange 4 sausage pieces and 1 cup potato mixture on center of each foil piece. Fold foil over sausage and potatoes so edges meet. Seal edges, making tight 1/2-inch fold; fold again. Allow space on sides for circulation and expansion.
3. Cover and grill packets 4 to 6 inches from medium-low heat 20 to 25 minutes, rotating packets 1/2 turn after 10 minutes, until potatoes are tender. Place packets on plates. Cut large × across each packet; fold back foil.

1 PACKET: Calories 415 (Calories from Fat 205); Fat 23g (Saturated 10g); Cholesterol 90mg; Sodium 1500mg; Carbohydrate 25g (Dietary Fiber 3g); Protein 27g • % Daily Value: Vitamin A 14%; Vitamin C 34%; Calcium 22%; Iron 8% • Exchanges: 1 1/2 Starch, 3 High-Fat Meat • Carbohydrate Choices: 1 1/2

together time

Place some white or brown paper on a picnic table, patio or deck, and let the kids color or paint while you're grilling. Weight the paper down with rocks if it's windy. Get out the paints, brushes or markers, and let the artists have a go at it!

Grilled Sausage and Cheddar Potato Packets

Beef and Bean Dinner

8 SERVINGS   PREP: 25 MIN   BAKE: 45 MIN

1 pound lean ground beef

1 medium onion, chopped (1/2 cup)

5 slices bacon

1 can (15 to 16 ounces) lima beans, drained

1 can (15 to 16 ounces) butter beans, drained

1 can (15 to 16 ounces) kidney beans, drained

1 can (28 ounces) baked beans

1/3 cup packed brown sugar

1/4 cup ketchup

2 tablespoons Worcestershire sauce

1. Heat oven to 350°. Cook beef and onion in 10-inch skillet over medium heat about 10 minutes, stirring occasionally, until brown; drain. Place beef mixture in ungreased 3-quart casserole.

2. Cook bacon in same skillet over low heat about 8 minutes, turning occasionally, until crisp and brown. Drain on paper towels; cool and crumble.

3. Stir beans, brown sugar, ketchup and Worcestershire sauce into beef in casserole. Top with bacon. Cover and bake 40 to 45 minutes or until hot and bubbly.

1 SERVING: Calories 425 (Calories from Fat 110); Fat 12g (Saturated 4g); Cholesterol 40mg; Sodium 1020mg; Carbohydrate 66g (Dietary Fiber 16g); Protein 30g • % Daily Value: Vitamin A 20%; Vitamin C 4%; Calcium 10%; Iron 48% • Exchanges: 4 1/2 Starch, 2 Very Lean Meat • Carbohydrate Choices: 4 1/2

together time

Use the slower pace of Sundays to plan a family dinner and set the table with all the trimmings. Then, when there's a more relaxed pace than the usual weeknight rush, everyone can be encouraged to use their best table manners.

Fiesta Taco Casserole

6 SERVINGS PREP: 15 MIN BAKE: 30 MIN

2 cups coarsely broken tortilla chips

1/2 recipe (about 4 1/3 cups) Kid-Pleasin' Chili (page 136), thawed if frozen, or two 15- to 16-ounce cans chili

1/2 cup reduced-fat sour cream

4 medium green onions, sliced (1/4 cup)

1 medium tomato, chopped (3/4 cup)

1 cup shredded Mexican, Cheddar or Monterey Jack cheese (4 ounces)

Additional tortilla chips, if desired

1. Heat oven to 350°. Place broken tortilla chips in ungreased 2-quart casserole. Top with chili. Dollop with sour cream; spread evenly. Sprinkle with onions, tomato and cheese.
2. Bake uncovered 20 to 30 minutes or until hot and bubbly. Arrange additional tortilla chips around edge of casserole.

1 SERVING: Calories 405 (Calories from Fat 170); Fat 19g (Saturated 9g); Cholesterol 70mg; Sodium 1120mg; Carbohydrate 37g (Dietary Fiber 6g); Protein 27g • % Daily Value: Vitamin A 30%; Vitamin C 16%; Calcium 16%; Iron 24% • Exchanges: 2 Starch, 1 Vegetable, 3 Medium-Fat Meat • Carbohydrate Choices: 2 1/2

together time

Make tasty bird snacks. Give each child a long piece of string or dental floss knotted at one end and threaded on a big, dull-pointed needle. String with fresh cranberries and popcorn. The finished strings look pretty and the birds will enjoy the fresh nibbles.

family fun BOOK NIGHT

Spark some good discussions and create a lifelong love of reading with a book night supper every once in a while. Family members can take turns selecting a book for all to read together. Let beginning readers read aloud to you while you're preparing dinner.

Menu

Dad's Fried Pan Fish (page 184)

Cheesy Breadstick Dunkers (at right)

Golden Raisin Slaw (at right)

Butterscotch Fish Cookies (at right)

Digital Vision

Cheesy Breadstick Dunkers

Heat oven to 375°. Unroll 1 can (7 ounces) **refrigerated soft breadsticks dough** (6 breadsticks), but do not separate. Place dough on ungreased cookie sheet. Top evenly with 3 tablespoons **shredded sharp Cheddar cheese**, 2 tablespoons **real bacon bits** and 1 tablespoon **Parmesan dry bread crumbs**. Bake 13 to 15 minutes or until golden brown. Cut into 6 long strips, then cut crosswise in half. Serve warm dipped in **pizza or pasta sauce**.

Golden Raisin Slaw

Toss one 16-ounce bag **coleslaw mix**, 2/3 cup **golden raisins** and 1/2 cup **salted sunflower nuts** in large bowl. Mix 1/3 cup **mayonnaise**, 1 1/2 tablespoons frozen (thawed) **orange juice concentrate** and 2 teaspoons **honey** in small bowl. Add to coleslaw mixture; toss.

Butterscotch Fish Cookies

Grease cookie sheet with butter. Heat 1 cup **butterscotch-flavored chips** and 1 tablespoon **shortening** in 3-quart saucepan over low heat, stirring constantly, until smooth; remove from heat. Stir in 1 package (6 ounces) **plain tiny fish-shaped crackers** and 1 cup **broken pretzel sticks** until well coated. Drop mixture by rounded tablespoonfuls onto cookie sheet; let stand until firm.

More Book Ideas

Let another book inspire you to try these recipes.

Barbecue Beef and Corn Shepherd's Pie (page 17)

Taco Shortcakes (page 110)

Grandma's Chicken Noodle Soup (page 100)

helping is fun

Mom or Dad

- Fries fish
- Shreds cheese and cuts breadsticks
- Heats butterscotch chips

The Kids

- Crush crackers and help bread fish
- Make slaw
- Stir in crackers and pretzels to make dessert

together time

To spark imaginations, match dinner to the book you're reading. For a fish dinner, read *The Rainbow Fish* by Marcus Pfister. Popcorn for a snack or dessert? Read *The Popcorn Dragon* by Jane Thayer.

Talk about everyone's favorite character or the most exciting part of the book. What are the scariest, saddest or happiest moments? **Act out the favorite character** in a fun game of charades.

Let each child take a turn telling his or her own ending to the story. You may be surprised with the creative changes to a story you all know well!

Start your own story and then have everyone add to it. The first person can begin with "once upon a time," then each family member continues the story. Decide how many rounds to go before you wrap up your tale.

Garlic Shepherd's Pie

6 SERVINGS PREP: 25 MIN BAKE: 30 MIN

- 1 pound ground beef
- 1 medium onion, chopped (1/2 cup)
- 2 cups frozen baby beans and carrots (from 1-pound bag)
- 1 cup sliced fresh mushrooms (3 ounces)
- 1 can (14 1/2 ounces) diced tomatoes, undrained
- 1 jar (12 ounces) beef gravy
- 2 tablespoons chili sauce
- 1/2 teaspoon dried basil leaves
- 1/8 teaspoon pepper
- 1/2 package (7.6-ounce size) roasted garlic mashed potatoes (1 pouch)
- 1 1/2 cups hot water
- 1/2 cup milk
- 2 teaspoons butter or margarine
- 2 teaspoons shredded Parmesan cheese

1. Heat oven to 350°. Cook beef and onion in 12-inch nonstick skillet over medium heat about 10 minutes, stirring occasionally, until beef is brown; drain well. Stir in frozen vegetables, mushrooms, tomatoes, gravy, chili sauce, basil and pepper. Heat to boiling; reduce heat. Cover and simmer about 10 minutes or until vegetables are tender.

2. Cook potatoes as directed on package for 4 servings, using 1 pouch potatoes and seasoning, hot water, milk and butter. Let stand 5 minutes.

3. Spoon beef mixture into ungreased square baking dish, 8 × 8 × 2 inches, or 2-quart casserole. Spoon potatoes onto beef mixture around edge of dish. Sprinkle with cheese. Bake uncovered 25 to 30 minutes or until potatoes are firm and beef mixture is bubbly.

1 SERVING: Calories 265 (Calories from Fat 135); Fat 15g (Saturated 6g); Cholesterol 50mg; Sodium 620mg; Carbohydrate 17g (Dietary Fiber 3g); Protein 19g • % Daily Value: Vitamin A 100%; Vitamin C 12%; Calcium 8%; Iron 14% • Exchanges: 1 Starch, 2 Medium-Fat Meat, 1 Fat • Carbohydrate Choices: 1

together time

Ask older kids to research the history of certain foods or customs. For instance, how did Shepherd's Pie get its name? What country did it come from? What ingredients are traditionally in it? Foods can reveal lots about other cultures.

Mini Italian Meat Loaves

6 SERVINGS PREP: 10 MIN BAKE: 32 MIN

1 1/2 pounds extra-lean ground beef

1/2 cup Italian-style dry bread crumbs

1/2 cup pepperoni-flavored pizza sauce (from 14-ounce jar)

1/4 teaspoon salt

1/4 teaspoon pepper

2 cloves garlic, finely chopped

1 egg

1/4 cup shredded Italian-style six-cheese blend or mozzarella cheese (1 ounce)

1. Heat oven to 350°. Spray 12 medium muffin cups, 2 1/2 × 1 1/4 inches, with cooking spray. Mix all ingredients except cheese in large bowl. Press beef mixture into muffin cups (cups will be very full). Place muffin pan on cookie sheet in oven to catch any spillover.
2. Bake about 30 minutes or until loaves are no longer pink in center and meat thermometer inserted in center of loaves in middle of muffin pan reads 160° (outer loaves will be done sooner).
3. Sprinkle 1 teaspoon cheese over each loaf. Bake 1 to 2 minutes longer or until cheese is melted. Immediately remove from cups. Serve with additional pizza sauce, heated, if desired.

1 SERVING: Calories 280 (Calories from Fat 145); Fat 16g (Saturated 6g); Cholesterol 105mg; Sodium 350mg; Carbohydrate 9g; (Dietary Fiber 1g); Protein 26g • % Daily Value: Vitamin A 4%; Vitamin C 4%; Calcium 6%; Iron 18% • Exchanges: 1/2 Starch, 3 1/2 Lean Meat, 1 Fat • Carbohydrate Choices: 1/2

together time

While preparing the meat loaves, place a chunk of tomato in one of them. The person who gets the meat loaf with the tomato wins a special surprise. Hint: The surprise could be for special time spent alone with a parent or a small toy.

Savory Beef Stew

6 SERVINGS PREP: 20 MIN BAKE: 3 HR 30 MIN

1 cup sun-dried tomatoes (not in oil)

1 1/2 pounds beef stew meat

1 medium onion, cut into 8 wedges

1 1/2 teaspoons seasoned salt

1 dried bay leaf

2 cups water

2 tablespoons all-purpose flour

12 small new potatoes (1 1/2 pounds), cut in half

1 bag (8 ounces) baby-cut carrots (about 30)

1. Heat oven to 325°. Cover dried tomatoes with boiling water. Let stand 10 minutes; drain and coarsely chop.
2. Mix tomatoes, beef, onion, seasoned salt and bay leaf in ovenproof 4-quart Dutch oven. Mix water and flour; stir into beef mixture. Cover and bake 2 hours, stirring once.
3. Stir in potatoes and carrots. Cover and bake 1 hour to 1 hour 30 minutes or until beef and vegetables are tender. Remove bay leaf.

1 SERVING: Calories 340 (Calories from Fat 125); Fat 14g (Saturated 5g); Cholesterol 70mg; Sodium 600mg; Carbohydrate 32g (Dietary Fiber 4g); Protein 27g • % Daily Value: Vitamin A 100%; Vitamin C 14%; Calcium 4%; Iron 26% • Exchanges: 2 Starch, 3 Lean Meat, 1/2 Fat • Carbohydrate Choices: 2

together time

Pile into the car after dinner during the holidays, and drive around the neighborhood to see the holiday lights and decorations. Why not sing a few carols at the same time?

Savory Beef Stew

Roasted Pork Chops and Vegetables

4 SERVINGS PREP: 20 MIN BAKE: 1 HR

2 teaspoons parsley flakes

1/2 teaspoon dried marjoram leaves

1/2 teaspoon dried thyme leaves

1/2 teaspoon garlic salt

1/4 teaspoon coarsely ground pepper

4 pork rib chops, 1/2 inch thick (1 pound), trimmed of fat

Olive oil-flavored cooking spray

6 new potatoes, cut into fourths (3 cups)

4 ounces mushrooms, cut in half (1 1/2 cups)

1 medium red bell pepper, cut into 1-inch pieces

1 medium onion, cut into thin wedges

1 medium tomato, cut into 8 wedges

1. Heat oven to 425°. Spray jelly roll pan, 15 1/2 × 10 1/2 × 1 inch, with cooking spray. Mix parsley, marjoram, thyme, garlic salt and pepper. Spray both sides of pork chops with cooking spray. Sprinkle with 1 to 1 1/2 teaspoons herb mixture. Place pork chop in each corner of pan.
2. Mix potatoes, mushrooms, bell pepper and onion in large bowl. Spray vegetables 2 or 3 times with cooking spray; stir. Sprinkle with remaining herb mixture; toss to coat. Spread evenly in center of pan.
3. Bake uncovered 45 minutes. Turn pork; stir vegetables. Place tomato wedges on vegetables. Bake uncovered 10 to 15 minutes longer or until pork is slightly pink when cut near bone and vegetables are tender.

1 SERVING: Calories 325 (Calories from Fat 65); Fat 7g (Saturated 2g); Cholesterol 55mg; Sodium 170mg; Carbohydrate 47g (Dietary Fiber 6g); Protein 25g • % Daily Value: Vitamin A 40%; Vitamin C 70%; Calcium 2%; Iron 18% • Exchanges: 2 1/2 Starch, 1 Vegetable, 3 Very Lean Meat • Carbohydrate Choices: 3

together time

Plan time together! Interacting with your kids in an enjoyable activity is a great way to stay in touch. As a group, come up with at least one activity that everyone can do together with a "weekend is here" attitude.

Baked Oregano Chicken

4 SERVINGS (plus 2 chicken breasts for another meal) PREP: 10 MIN BAKE: 25 MIN

1/4 cup dry bread crumbs

2 tablespoons grated Parmesan cheese

1/4 teaspoon dried oregano leaves

1/8 teaspoon garlic salt

1/8 teaspoon pepper

1/4 cup Dijon mustard

6 boneless, skinless chicken breast halves (about 1 3/4 pounds)

1. Heat oven to 425°. Spray jelly roll pan, 15 1/2 × 10 1/2 × 1 inch, with cooking spray.
2. Mix bread crumbs, cheese, oregano, garlic salt and pepper. Spread mustard on all sides of 4 chicken breasts. Cover mustard-coated chicken breasts with bread crumb mixture. Place all 6 chicken breasts in pan.
3. Bake uncovered about 25 minutes or until juice of chicken is no longer pink when centers of thickest pieces are cut. Cover and refrigerate the 2 uncoated chicken breasts.

1 SERVING: Calories 175 (Calories from Fat 45); Fat 5g (Saturated 2g); Cholesterol 75mg; Sodium 410mg; Carbohydrate 4g (Dietary Fiber 0g); Protein 28g • % Daily Value: Vitamin A 0%; Vitamin C 0%; Calcium 6%; Iron 6% • Exchanges: 4 Very Lean Meat, 1 Fat • Carbohydrate Choices: 0

together time

Decorate baked cookies or cupcakes. Start with home-baked or bakery-made cookies or cupcakes. Let each child have a plastic knife to spread frosting, then sprinkle on colorful toppings.

Chicken Spaghetti Olé

6 SERVINGS PREP: 25 MIN BAKE: 30 MIN

6 ounces uncooked spaghetti

1 tablespoon butter or margarine

1 small green bell pepper, chopped (1/2 cup)

1 medium stalk celery, chopped (1/2 cup)

1 small onion, chopped (1/4 cup)

1 can (10 ounces) diced tomatoes and mild green chiles, undrained

1 can (8 ounces) tomato sauce

1 package (8 ounces) process cheese spread loaf, cut into cubes

1/2 teaspoon salt

1/4 teaspoon pepper

2 cups diced cooked chicken or turkey

Sliced jalepeño chilies, if desired

1. Heat oven to 350°. Spray rectangular baking dish, 13 × 9 × 2 inches, with cooking spray. Cook and drain spaghetti as directed on package.

2. While spaghetti is cooking, melt butter in 12-inch skillet over medium heat. Cook bell pepper, celery and onion in butter, stirring occasionally, until tender. Stir in tomatoes, tomato sauce, cheese, salt and pepper; reduce heat to low. Heat, stirring frequently, until cheese is melted.

3. Stir in chicken and spaghetti. Spoon into baking dish. Bake uncovered about 30 minutes or until bubbly around edges. Top with chilies.

1 SERVING: Calories 380 (Calories from Fat 160); Fat 18g (Saturated 10g); Cholesterol 85mg; Sodium 1170mg; Carbohydrate 32g (Dietary Fiber 3g); Protein 26g • % Daily Value: Vitamin A 20%; Vitamin C 18%; Calcium 22%; Iron 14% • Exchanges: 2 Starch, 3 Medium-Fat Meat • Carbohydrate Choices: 2

together time

Give your family a tasty reminder of summer. Serve corn on the cob and sliced cucumbers in the winter. You'll find ready-to-cook fresh ears of corn in the produce or frozen food section of your supermarket, and cucumbers are available in the produce section all year-round. What a fresh treat!

Mom's Homey Chicken Soup

6 SERVINGS PREP: 15 MIN COOK: 30 MIN

3 cups homemade or canned chicken broth

3 cups water

1 cup baby-cut carrots

2 medium stalks celery, sliced (1 cup)

1 medium onion, chopped (1/2 cup)

2 cloves garlic, finely chopped

2 tablespoons chicken bouillon granules

1 tablespoon chopped fresh parsley

1 tablespoon chopped fresh or 1 teaspoon dried thyme leaves

1 cup frozen egg noodles (from 12-ounce bag)

2 cups cut-up cooked chicken

1. Heat all ingredients except noodles and chicken to boiling in 4-quart Dutch oven.
2. Stir in noodles; reduce heat. Simmer uncovered 20 to 25 minutes, adding chicken to Dutch oven for last 5 minutes, until vegetables and noodles are tender.

1 SERVING: Calories 220 (Calories from Fat 55); Fat 6g (Saturated 1g); Cholesterol 50mg; Sodium 3290mg; Carbohydrate 21g (Dietary Fiber 2g); Protein 22g • % Daily Value: Vitamin A 80%; Vitamin C 8%; Calcium 6%; Iron 12% • Exchanges: 1 Starch, 2 Very Lean Meat, 1 Vegetable, 1 Fat • Carbohydrate Choices: 1 1/2

together time

Have kids create 3-D picture frames for their artwork. Glue 4 wooden sticks with rounded ends to a piece of paper, one on each side, to create the frame. Then kids can draw a picture and glue it in place inside the frame.

Turkey and Ham Tetrazzini

6 SERVINGS PREP: 15 MIN BAKE: 35 MIN

1 package (9 ounces) refrigerated linguine

1 can (10 3/4 ounces) condensed cream of mushroom soup

1 can (10 3/4 ounces) condensed cream of chicken soup

3/4 cup milk

2 tablespoons dry white wine or apple juice

2 cups cut-up cooked turkey or chicken

1/2 cup cut-up fully cooked smoked ham

1 small green bell pepper, chopped (1/2 cup)

1/4 cup halved pitted ripe olives

1/2 cup grated Parmesan cheese

1/4 cup slivered almonds, toasted

1. Heat oven to 375°. Cook and drain linguine as directed on package.
2. While linguine is cooking, mix soups, milk and wine in ungreased 2-quart casserole. Stir in linguine, turkey, ham, bell pepper and olives. Sprinkle with cheese.
3. Bake uncovered about 35 minutes or until hot and bubbly. Sprinkle with almonds.

1 SERVING: Calories 330 (Calories from Fat 145); Fat 16g (Saturated 5g); Cholesterol 55mg; Sodium 980mg; Carbohydrate 24g (Dietary Fiber 2g); Protein 23g • % Daily Value: Vitamin A 8%; Vitamin C 8%; Calcium 20%; Iron 12% • Exchanges: 1 1/2 Starch, 2 1/2 Medium-Fat Meat, 1/2 Fat • Carbohydrate Choices: 1 1/2

together time

Get creative! Food arranged in artistic patterns looks as good as it tastes! Arrange sliced fruits and vegetables on a platter, with cucumber, zucchini or green bell peppers on the outside and grape or cherry tomatoes and baby carrots on the inside.

Turkey and Ham Tetrazzini

Crunchy Garlic Chicken

6 SERVINGS PREP: 10 MIN BAKE: 25 MIN

2 tablespoons butter or margarine, melted

2 tablespoons milk

1 tablespoon chopped fresh chives

1/2 teaspoon salt

1/2 teaspoon garlic powder

2 cups cornflakes cereal, crushed (1 cup)

3 tablespoons chopped fresh parsley

1/2 teaspoon paprika

6 boneless, skinless chicken breast halves (about 1 3/4 pounds)

2 tablespoons butter or margarine, melted

1. Heat oven to 425°. Spray rectangular pan, 13 × 9 × 2 inches, with cooking spray.

2. Mix 2 tablespoons butter, the milk, chives, salt and garlic powder in shallow bowl. Mix crushed cereal, parsley and paprika in another shallow bowl. Dip chicken into milk mixture, then coat lightly and evenly with cereal mixture. Place in pan. Drizzle with 2 tablespoons butter.

3. Bake uncovered 20 to 25 minutes or until chicken is no longer pink when centers of thickest pieces are cut.

1 SERVING: Calories 255 (Calories from Fat 110); Fat 12g (Saturated 6g); Cholesterol 95mg; Sodium 410mg; Carbohydrate 9g (Dietary Fiber 0g); Protein 28g • % Daily Value: Vitamin A 14%; Vitamin C 6%; Calcium 4%; Iron 20% • Exchanges: 1/2 Starch, 4 Lean Meat • Carbohydrate Choices: 1/2

together time

Make a bird feeder with leftover bread that's too crusty to eat. Tie string around the slices, package style, leaving enough string to tie the ends to a tree branch or clothes-line. See what different kinds of birds come to eat!

Chicken Alfredo Pot Pie

6 SERVINGS PREP: 15 MIN BAKE: 30 MIN

1 can (11 ounces) refrigerated soft breadsticks

1 jar (16 ounces) Alfredo pasta sauce

1/3 cup milk

1 bag (1 pound) frozen broccoli, cauliflower and carrots, thawed and drained

2 cups cut-up cooked chicken

2 tablespoons grated Parmesan cheese

1 teaspoon Italian seasoning

1. Heat oven to 375°. Unroll breadstick dough; separate at perforations to form 12 strips and set aside.

2. Mix pasta sauce, milk, vegetables and chicken in 3-quart saucepan. Heat to boiling, stirring occasionally. Spoon into ungreased rectangular pan, 13 × 9 × 2 inches.

3. Twist each dough strip; arrange crosswise over hot chicken mixture, gently stretching strips if necessary to fit. Sprinkle with cheese and Italian seasoning.

4. Bake uncovered 20 to 30 minutes or until breadsticks are deep golden brown.

1 SERVING: Calories 525 (Calories from Fat 290); Fat 32g (Saturated 18g); Cholesterol 120mg; Sodium 750mg; Carbohydrate 36g (Dietary Fiber 4g); Protein 27g • % Daily Value: Vitamin A 60%; Vitamin C 20%; Calcium 32%; Iron 14% • Exchanges: 2 Starch, 1 Vegetable, 3 High-Fat Meat, 1 Fat • Carbohydrate Choices: 2 1/2

together time

Keep the kids eating their vegetables by letting them dip or dunk veggies into melted cheese sauce or ranch dressing. Some great dippers? Sliced red and green bell peppers, baby carrots, broccoli, cauliflower and celery sticks.

Home-Style Chicken Dinner

4 SERVINGS PREP: 5 MIN COOK: 30 MIN

1 tablespoon butter or margarine

4 boneless, skinless chicken breast halves (about 1 1/4 pounds)

1/2 teaspoon salt

1/4 teaspoon pepper, if desired

3/4 cup water

1 envelope (0.87 ounce) chicken gravy mix

1 bag (14 ounces) frozen baby whole potatoes, broccoli, carrots, baby corn and red pepper strips

1 jar (4.5 ounces) sliced mushrooms, drained

Chopped fresh chives or parsley, if desired

1. Melt butter in 10-inch nonstick skillet over medium heat. Sprinkle chicken with salt and pepper. Cook chicken in butter 15 to 20 minutes, turning once, until juice is no longer pink when centers of thickest pieces are cut. Remove chicken from skillet; keep warm.
2. Mix water and gravy mix (dry) in small bowl; pour into same skillet. Stir in frozen vegetables and mushrooms. Heat to boiling; reduce heat. Simmer uncovered about 5 minutes, stirring occasionally, until largest pieces of potato are hot. Add chicken; cover and simmer about 2 minutes or until chicken is heated through.
3. Serve vegetable and gravy mixture over chicken. Sprinkle with chives.

1 SERVING: Calories 265 (Calories from Fat 70); Fat 8g (Saturated 3g); Cholesterol 95mg; Sodium 880mg; Carbohydrate 19g (Dietary Fiber 3g); Protein 30g • % Daily Value: Vitamin A 100%; Vitamin C 32%; Calcium 4%; Iron 10% • Exchanges: 1 Starch, 1 Vegetable, 3 1/2 Very Lean Meat, 1 Fat • Carbohydrate Choices: 1

together time

Celebrate TGIF-NC! That's "Thank Goodness It's the Family's Night to Cook! On this night, give the regular cook the night off, and let the whole family be in charge of planning, shopping, preparing, cleaning up—or even just ordering in dinner.

Home-Style Chicken Dinner

Mom's Macaroni and Cheese

5 SERVINGS PREP: 25 MIN BAKE: 30 MIN

1 1/2 cups uncooked elbow macaroni (5 ounces)

2 tablespoons butter or margarine

1 small onion, chopped (1/4 cup)

1/2 teaspoon salt

1/4 teaspoon pepper

1/4 cup all-purpose flour

1 3/4 cups milk

6 ounces process American cheese loaf, cut into 1/2-inch cubes

1. Heat oven to 375°. Cook and drain macaroni as directed on package.
2. While macaroni is cooking, melt butter in 2-quart saucepan over medium heat. Cook onion, salt and pepper in butter, stirring occasionally, until onion is crisp-tender. Mix flour and milk until smooth; stir into onion mixture. Heat to boiling, stirring constantly. Boil and stir 1 minute; remove from heat. Stir in cheese until melted. Stir in macaroni.
3. Spoon macaroni mixture into ungreased 1 1/2-quart casserole. Bake uncovered about 30 minutes or until bubbly and light brown.

1 SERVING: Calories 345 (Calories from Fat 150); Fat 17g (Saturated 11g); Cholesterol 50mg; Sodium 800mg; Carbohydrate 33g (Dietary Fiber 1g); Protein 15g • % Daily Value: Vitamin A 16%; Vitamin C 0%; Calcium 28%; Iron 8% • Exchanges: 2 Starch, 1 High-Fat Meat, 2 Fat • Carbohydrate Choices: 2

together time

After a simple, tasty meal, serve a simple dessert. Spread chocolate frosting or peanut butter or both on graham crackers. Put crackers together to make chocolate-graham or chocolate-peanut butter-graham sandwiches.

Zesty Roasted Chicken and Potatoes

6 SERVINGS PREP: 12 MIN BAKE: 55 MIN

6 boneless, skinless chicken breast halves (about 1 3/4 pounds)

1/2 teaspoon salt

1/3 cup mayonnaise or salad dressing

3 tablespoons Dijon or spicy brown mustard

1/2 teaspoon pepper

2 cloves garlic, finely chopped

1 pound new potatoes, each cut into 6 wedges

Chopped fresh chives, if desired

1. Heat oven to 350°. Line broiler pan with aluminum foil. Spray rack of broiler pan with cooking spray. Arrange chicken on center of rack in broiler pan; sprinkle both sides with salt.
2. Mix mayonnaise, mustard, pepper and garlic in large bowl; brush about 3 tablespoons mixture on chicken. Add potatoes to remaining mayonnaise mixture; toss. Arrange potatoes around chicken.
3. Bake uncovered 45 to 55 minutes, turning potatoes halfway through cooking, until juice of chicken is no longer pink when centers of thickest pieces are cut and potatoes are tender. Sprinkle with chives.

1 SERVING: Calories 300 (Calories from Fat 115); Fat 13g (Saturated 3g); Cholesterol 80mg; Sodium 520mg; Carbohydrate 16g; (Dietary Fiber 2g); Protein 29g • % Daily Value: Vitamin A 0%; Vitamin C 6%; Calcium 2%; Iron 10% • Exchanges: 1 Starch, 4 Lean Meat • Carbohydrate Choices: 1

together time

Ask your kids to tell you what happened in school today. Experts say that when parents stay involved, kids are happier and more likely to do well in school.

Lemony Fish over Vegetables and Rice

4 SERVINGS PREP: 10 MIN COOK: 23 MIN

- 1 package (6.1 ounces) fried rice (rice and vermicelli mix with almonds and Oriental seasonings)
- 2 tablespoons butter or margarine
- 2 cups water
- 1/2 teaspoon grated lemon peel
- 1 bag (1 pound) frozen corn, broccoli and red peppers
- 1 pound mild-flavored fish fillets (such as cod, flounder, haddock, halibut, orange roughy or sole), about 1/2 inch thick
- 1/2 teaspoon lemon pepper
- 1 tablespoon lemon juice
- 2 tablespoons chopped fresh parsley

1. Cook rice and butter in 12-inch nonstick skillet over medium heat 2 to 3 minutes, stirring occasionally, until rice is golden brown. Stir in water, seasoning packet from rice mix and lemon peel. Heat to boiling; reduce heat. Cover and simmer 10 minutes.
2. Stir in frozen vegetables. Heat to boiling, stirring occasionally. Cut fish into 4 serving pieces; arrange on rice mixture. Sprinkle fish with lemon pepper; drizzle with lemon juice. Reduce heat.
3. Cover and simmer 8 to 10 minutes or until fish flakes easily with fork and vegetables are tender. Sprinkle with parsley.

1 SERVING: Calories 255 (Calories from Fat 65); Fat 7g (Saturated 4g); Cholesterol 75mg; Sodium 320mg; Carbohydrate 22g (Dietary Fiber 3g); Protein 26g • % Daily Value: Vitamin A 64%; Vitamin C 72%; Calcium 4%; Iron 8% • Exchanges: 1 Starch, 1 Vegetable, 3 Very Lean Meat, 1 Fat • Carbohydrate Choices: 1 1/2

together time

Volunteer time to the family. Have each family member write on 3 × 5-inch note cards what they will volunteer to do. Perhaps "This card entitles you to spend the day with only me at the movies" or "I will help you clean the kitchen next week" or "I will help you wash the car next Saturday."

Lemony Fish over
Vegetables and Rice

Dad's Fried Pan Fish

6 SERVINGS PREP: 15 MIN COOK: 20 MIN

Oil for frying

1 1/2 cups round buttery cracker crumbs (40 crackers)

1/3 cup sliced almonds

2 eggs

1 tablespoon water

1/2 cup all-purpose flour

2 pounds walleye pike, sole or other delicate fish fillets or other pan fish fillets

1 teaspoon salt

1/2 teaspoon pepper

1. Heat 1/4 inch of oil in 12-inch skillet over medium-high heat until hot. Mix cracker crumbs and almonds in shallow pan. Beat eggs in another shallow pan with fork or wire whisk. Add water to eggs; beat well. Place flour in third shallow pan.
2. Sprinkle fish fillets with salt and pepper. Dip into flour, then into egg mixture. Coat with cracker crumb mixture.
3. Place fillets, a few at a time, in hot oil. Cook 3 to 5 minutes, turning 3 or 4 times, until golden brown. Drain on several layers of paper towels.

1 SERVING: Calories 355 (Calories from Fat 170); Fat 19g (Saturated 3g); Cholesterol 135mg; Sodium 550mg; Carbohydrate 15g (Dietary Fiber 1g); Protein 31g • % Daily Value: Vitamin A 2%; Vitamin C 0%; Calcium 4%; Iron 8% • Exchanges: 1 Starch, 4 Lean Meat, 1 Fat • Carbohydrate Choices: 1

together time

Set aside time on Sundays for family activities. Let the kids choose an activity that they enjoy, perhaps playing a board game or a card game at home or going out for miniature golf or bowling.

Crab and Spinach Casserole

4 SERVINGS PREP: 15 MIN BAKE: 20 MIN

2 cups uncooked gemelli (twist) pasta (8 ounces)

1 package (1.8 ounces) leek soup mix

2 cups milk

1 package (8 ounces) refrigerated imitation crabmeat chunks or 1 cup cut-up cooked chicken

2 cups baby spinach leaves

1/4 cup freshly shredded Parmesan cheese

1. Heat oven to 350°. Spray 1 1/2-quart casserole or square baking dish, 8 × 8 × 2 inches, with cooking spray. Cook and drain pasta as directed on package.
2. While pasta is cooking, mix soup mix (dry) and milk in 1-quart saucepan. Heat to boiling, stirring constantly.
3. Cut up larger pieces of crabmeat if desired. Mix pasta, crabmeat and spinach in baking dish. Pour soup mixture over pasta mixture; stir gently to mix. Spread evenly. Sprinkle with cheese.
4. Bake uncovered about 20 minutes or until bubbly and light golden brown.

1 SERVING: **Calories 400 (Calories from Fat 55); Fat 6g (Saturated 3g); Cholesterol 30mg; Sodium 1780mg; Carbohydrate 63g (Dietary Fiber 3g); Protein 24g • % Daily Value: Vitamin A 34%; Vitamin C 8%; Calcium 28%; Iron 16% • Exchanges: 3 1/2 Starch, 1/2 Milk, 1 Vegetable, 1 1/2 Very Lean Meat • Carbohydrate Choices: 4**

together time

Get to know your kids' friends by inviting them, one at a time, for dinner. Plan a simple, fun activity during dinner and have a "top-your-own" dessert. There may even be a little time afterward for a board game or two.

Helpful Nutrition and Cooking Information

Nutrition Guidelines

We provide nutrition information for each recipe that includes calories, fat, cholesterol, sodium, carbohydrate, fiber and protein. Individual food choices can be based on this information.

Recommended intake for a daily diet of 2,000 calories as set by the Food and Drug Administration

Total Fat	Less than 65g
Saturated Fat	Less than 20g
Cholesterol	Less than 300mg
Sodium	Less than 2,400mg
Total Carbohydrate	300g
Dietary Fiber	25g

Criteria Used for Calculating Nutrition Information

- The first ingredient was used wherever a choice is given (such as 1/3 cup sour cream or plain yogurt).
- The first ingredient amount was used wherever a range is given (such as 3- to 3 1/2- pound cut-up broiler-fryer chicken).
- The first serving number was used wherever a range is given (such as 4 to 6 servings).
- "If desired" ingredients and recipe variations were not included (such as sprinkle with brown sugar, if desired).
- Only the amount of a marinade or frying oil that is estimated to be absorbed by the food during preparation or cooking was calculated.

Ingredients Used in Recipe Testing and Nutrition Calculations

- Ingredients used for testing represent those that the majority of consumers use in their homes: large eggs, 2% milk, 80%-lean ground beef, canned ready-to-use chicken broth and vegetable oil spread containing not less than 65% fat.
- Fat-free, low-fat or low-sodium products were not used, unless otherwise indicated.
- Solid vegetable shortening (not butter, margarine, nonstick cooking sprays or vegetable oil spread as they can cause sticking problems) was used to grease pans, unless otherwise indicated.

Equipment Used in Recipe Testing

We use equipment for testing that the majority of consumers use in their homes. If a specific piece of equipment (such as a wire whisk) is necessary for recipe success, it is listed in the recipe.

- Cookware and bakeware without nonstick coatings were used, unless otherwise indicated.
- No dark-colored, black or insulated bakeware was used.
- When a pan is specified in a recipe, a metal pan was used; a baking dish or pie plate means ovenproof glass was used.
- An electric hand mixer was used for mixing only when mixer speeds are specified in the recipe directions. When a mixer speed is not given, a spoon or fork was used.

Cooking Terms Glossary

Beat: Mix ingredients vigorously with spoon, fork, wire whisk, hand beater or electric mixer until smooth and uniform.

Boil: Heat liquid until bubbles rise continuously and break on the surface and steam is given off. For rolling boil, the bubbles form rapidly.

Chop: Cut into coarse or fine irregular pieces with a knife, food chopper, blender or food processor.

Cube: Cut into squares 1/2 inch or larger.

Dice: Cut into squares smaller than 1/2 inch.

Grate: Cut into tiny particles using small rough holes of grater (citrus peel or chocolate).

Grease: Rub the inside surface of a pan with shortening, using pastry brush, piece of waxed paper or paper towel, to prevent food from sticking during baking (as for some casseroles).

Julienne: Cut into thin, matchlike strips, using knife or food processor (vegetables, fruits, meats).

Mix: Combine ingredients in any way that distributes them evenly.

Sauté: Cook foods in hot oil over medium-high heat with frequent tossing and turning motion.

Shred: Cut into long thin pieces by rubbing food across the holes of a shredder, as for cheese, or by using a knife to slice very thinly, as for cabbage.

Simmer: Cook in liquid just below the boiling point on top of the stove; usually after reducing heat from a boil. Bubbles will rise slowly and break just below the surface.

Stir: Mix ingredients until uniform consistency. Stir once in a while for stirring occasionally, often for stirring frequently and continuously for stirring constantly.

Toss: Tumble ingredients (such as green salad) lightly with a lifting motion, usually to coat evenly or mix with another food.

Metric Conversion Guide

Volume

U.S. Units	Canadian Metric	Australian Metric
1/4 teaspoon	1 mL	1 ml
1/2 teaspoon	2 mL	2 ml
1 teaspoon	5 mL	5 ml
1 tablespoon	15 mL	20 ml
1/4 cup	50 mL	60 ml
1/3 cup	75 mL	80 ml
1/2 cup	125 mL	125 ml
2/3 cup	150 mL	170 ml
3/4 cup	175 mL	190 ml
1 cup	250 mL	250 ml
1 quart	1 liter	1 liter
1 1/2 quarts	1.5 liters	1.5 liters
2 quarts	2 liters	2 liters
2 1/2 quarts	2.5 liters	2.5 liters
3 quarts	3 liters	3 liters
4 quarts	4 liters	4 liters

Weight

U.S. Units	Canadian Metric	Australian Metric
1 ounce	30 grams	30 grams
2 ounces	55 grams	60 grams
3 ounces	85 grams	90 grams
4 ounces (1/4 pound)	115 grams	125 grams
8 ounces (1/2 pound)	225 grams	225 grams
16 ounces (1 pound)	455 grams	500 grams
1 pound	455 grams	1/2 kilogram

Measurements

Inches	Centimeters
1	2.5
2	5.0
3	7.5
4	10.0
5	12.5
6	15.0
7	17.5
8	20.5
9	23.0
10	25.5
11	28.0
12	30.5
13	33.0

Temperatures

Fahrenheit	Celsius
32°	0°
212°	100°
250°	120°
275°	140°
300°	150°
325°	160°
350°	180°
375°	190°
400°	200°
425°	220°
450°	230°
475°	240°
500°	260°

Note: The recipes in this cookbook have not been developed or tested using metric measures. When converting recipes to metric, some variations in quality may be noted.

Index

Page numbers in ***bold italics*** indicate a photograph.